DIAGNOSING THE HEART OF YOUR CHURCH

How Church Leaders Can Assess Systemic Corporate Dysfunction

By Mark Barnard

August 2015

Copyright © 2015 Mark Barnard

All Scripture quotations taken from the New American Standard Bible, unless otherwise noted.

All rights reserved.

ISBN-10: 1516945077
ISBN-13: 978-1516945078

DEDICATION

To our friends and supporters whose prayers, encouragement, and generosity have helped to make this ministry possible.
Thank you!

TABLE OF CONTENTS

	Foreword	vii
	Introduction	xi
1	Finding the Right Tool	1
2	The Biblical Roots of Church Growth/Church Health Teaching	9
3	The Biblical Roots of a Church's Systemic Health	17
4	The Five Spheres of a Church's Systemic Health	29
5	Sphere 1 – The Corporate Pulse	35
6	Sphere 2 – Trust in Leadership	43
7	Sphere 3 – Mission/Vision Fulfillment	53
8	Sphere 4 - Communication	63
9	Sphere 5 – Historical Wounds	71
10	ChurchScan Inventory	83
	Other Resources	101
	Acknowledgements	103
	About the Author - Contact Us	105

FOREWORD

In 1994, during one of the most stressful periods of my life as a pastor, my wife Diane was diagnosed as having a blockage of her "left main-stem artery," the one that covers the back two-thirds of the heart muscle. Her cardiologist told her that this blockage was so serious (90%) that it was a wonder she was still alive, because with that much of a major artery blocked, carrying a laundry basket was enough to put one into a fatal cardiac arrest.

We had no idea. We knew something was not right as she was experiencing tightness in her chest and shortness of breath for the slightest exertion. Diane was a young woman for such a diagnosis (43), but then she began to learn that this was a genetic problem on her father's side. She had three of her father's brothers who dropped dead of cardiac arrests in their early forties, a deadly legacy through her paternal DNA.

She was fortunate though to have had a personal physician who listened to her and who was sensitive to the things she was feeling, who knew the right questions to ask and did not rule things out because of Diane's age. We give credit to God and that doctor for saving her life, even if she (the doctor) herself didn't perform the surgery.

What was happening with my wife was mirrored in my church at that time—it was and had been experiencing pain in several specific areas. But we, I as pastor along with my elders and staff, had no idea how to diagnose what we were seeing or experiencing, but believe me we tried. There had not been a seminary class on the subject, nor anything in the set of church growth/church health books we scoured.

Then, in one of those inimitable moments of Divine mercy and grace, I actually started a doctoral program with the aim of extracting myself from pastoral ministry, having reached what I believed was my limit of pain and frustration. However, the course work got me to studying the arc of my own life and how I had been left with painful legacies from my lineage, things I was now responsible to overcome to follow Christ fully. In some of the scariest moments of my life but with Christ fully beside me, I faced the dark legacies of my background, and, after 17 years of ministry, finally grew up and received healing in some much needed areas.

Watching the power of divine healing from the futile way of life I had inherited from my forefathers, I wondered if God could do the same thing for a church which was in such obvious pain. The challenge here though was the same one I faced (in the context of my family) and my wife faced (in the context of her physical body), which is a proper diagnosis. Healing therapy only works if the diagnosis has been made correctly.

Mark Barnard, my partner at Blessing Point Ministries, has written a book to help the pastor, board, or district denominational leader know how to properly diagnose a church which is experiencing painful symptoms. This is "outside-the-box thinking" for most church leaders, moving away from the programmatic approach to fixing ministry and understanding the church body to be a living thing which can carry pain for decades as a response to Divine discipline which it has failed to understand.

If you feel you have tried *everything* to turn your church around and none of it has worked, then we encourage you to shift paradigms and look at your church differently. Mark will challenge you to evaluate your church in five key areas that are the true measure of corporate spiritual health, diagnose your situation in a much more

FOREWORD

biblical way, and offer biblical responses to what you may discover that can provide the hope of deep and lasting corporate healing.

That is our hope and prayer for all of God's churches today.

Dr. Kenneth Quick
Associate Professor, Capital Seminary and Graduate School
Director of Consulting
Blessing Point Ministries

INTRODUCTION

Perhaps you've heard the story about a group of twenty bootleggers who were rounded up during Prohibition days. The Sheriff hauled them all in before the Judge. The Judge questioned each man in turn, asking his name, address, and occupation. When it came to their occupations nineteen of the bootleggers claimed to be "consultants." Incredulous, the judge asked the last man, "Are you a consultant *too*?" The man replied, "No your honor, *I am a bootlegger*." Stunned by the defendant's honesty the judge went on to ask, "Well then, how's business?" The forthright bootlegger replied, "Your Honor, it'd be a lot better if there weren't so many consultants around!"

I am a consultant. And let's face it. There are lots of consultants working with local churches today. At Blessing Point Ministries we work with one particular aspect of church life. We endeavor to bring healing to congregations that have been negatively impacted by corporate pain. When I share what I do with church people they often reply with something like, "You've got great job security!" It's true. There appears to be no shortage of churches facing one kind of major crisis or another. Just about every Christian has been part of a church that was in pain or caused it. The need *is* great. But one thing we've discovered is that churches are slow to ask for help, even when their pain is off the charts.

Reading *Diagnosing the Heart of Your Church*, which challenges leaders to take a hard look at the systemic health of their churches, may generate pain too - at least initially. Why? Because measuring a church's *systemic* health means going beyond the *apparent* condition of your church. Systemic functioning relates to spiritual and relational dynamics that operate behind the scenes (and have operated historically) in the body of a church. When we talk about measuring or diagnosing the level of "systemic health" we assess things that tend to spread through and affect the whole congregational body. These dynamics will reshape the culture of a church if they go unattended. Many pastors and church leaders ignore the ramifications of such underlying spiritual and relational issues. Such grave oversight (or perhaps better, "under-sight") always proves costly.

Diagnosing the Heart of Your Church is designed to help you ask the right questions, questions leaders need to discuss candidly. It alerts you to areas of church life that need strengthening. It helps you recognize if you simply have a problem in one area or if an unseen infection has spread through your church body. Most importantly it offers you a tool to assess your congregation's true health.

When is it a good time to diagnose the heart of your church? If you're a pastor and new to your congregation, this would be a great time to evaluate the systemic health of your church. Why not take a look "under the hood" *before* you embark on a new missional journey? If your church is in transition, why not take time to reflect on your church's true state? It might be just the time to deal with underlying problems *before* calling a new shepherd. If your church is in the midst of crisis, this book helps you understand some of the causes of your corporate pain. Why risk *repeating* the same old problems? And if you want to protect the health of your church, this book reveals the kinds of concerns to which you must be alert. *Forewarned* is forearmed!

Should you discover that your church needs healing from the kinds of systemic problems I describe, I trust you'll set your church on the path of healing. The next book in this series, *Healing the Heart of Your Church,* written by my good friend and partner in ministry Dr.

INTRODUCTION

Kenneth Quick, lays out a process for churches to heal the corporate pain Jesus longs for them to treat. In some cases it's a process a church can undertake on its own. In other cases it's best to bring in one of those "consultants" I mention above. If the latter proves to be the case, we hope you'll invite us to walk alongside your church for a time. Together we'll work to discern the Great Physician's prescription for your congregation. Visit www.blessingpoint.org to learn how we can help you *diagnose*, *heal*, and *sustain* the heart of your church.

For the restored radiance of His Bride,

Rev. Mark Barnard, President
Blessing Point Ministries
Ephesians 5:27

CHAPTER 1

Finding the Right Tool

The story goes, "A German machine tool company once developed a very fine bit for drilling holes in steel. The tiny bit could bore a hole about the size of a human hair. This seemed like a tremendously valuable innovation. The Germans sent samples off to Russia, the United States, and Japan, suggesting that this bit was the ultimate in machining technology.

From the Russians, they heard nothing. From the Americans came a quick response inquiring as to the price of the bits, available discounts, and the possibility of a licensing arrangement. After some delay, there was the predictable, polite response from the Japanese, complementing the Germans on their achievement, but with a postscript noting that the Germans' bit was enclosed with a slight alteration. Excitedly, the German engineers opened the package, carefully examined their bit, and to their amazement discovered that the Japanese had bored a neat hole through it."[1]

Behind this story lays the assumption that a better drill bit will change the world! Pastors and local church leaders *want* a better drill bit too. They want the tool that turns things around, bringing life to a declining church. They search for the innovation which restores cohesiveness to the disgruntled staff of a mega church. In a heartbeat, they'll order the gizmo that stimulates growth in a church that lingers on life support. Church leaders grasp at the latest book, training, or speaker who promises *results*. The fact that

---

[1] Max DePree, *Leadership Jazz* (New York: Doubleday, 1992) 14-15.

over one million copies of Rick Warren's book, *The Purpose Driven Church*, have been sold worldwide, demonstrates that church leaders *want* solutions.

Because, biblically, the church is described as a body, untreated problems rarely remain isolated in one part or member. Unaddressed illnesses in the local church tend to spread over time through the whole body, affecting the church as a *system*. Warren himself alludes to this when he refers to the various diseases[2] churches contract and that churches need to be "brought back into balance" before they can grow.[3] Unfortunately, for the 80%-90% of American churches currently *out* of balance, approaches that fail to address a church's systemic functioning get short term results at best.[4]

THE WRONG TOOL

When I was a kid, I mowed lawns to make money. One day, a lady I worked for tried to expand my duties to include those of an arborist. She asked me to climb a tree in her front yard and cut down a particular branch which she felt needed to be removed. Sounded good to me! Any day I had permission to climb a tree was a good day, especially if I was getting paid. So I borrowed a hand saw from the man across the street and up I went. I cut my way through most of the limb, but could not free the branch from its trunk. Frustrated, I decided to try another approach. I used the handle of the saw as a hammer and tried to beat the branch into submission. It wasn't long before the neighbor man, to whom the saw belonged, observed my method and yelled, "Hey kid, what are you doing with my saw? That's *not* a hammer!"

---

[2] See *The Eighth Letter* by Mark Barnard and Ken Quick to discover how Jesus addresses and deals with corporate diseases in Rev. 2-3.
[3] Rick Warren, *The Purpose Driven Church* (Grand Rapids: Zondervan, 1995) 16.
[4] Most church growth/health leaders estimate that 80%-90% of American churches are stagnant or declining.

FINDING THE RIGHT TOOL

Maybe I needed a hammer, maybe I didn't. Maybe I really needed a chainsaw. Or, perhaps there was a problem with the whole idea of a 12 year old boy in a tree with a saw! There comes a time when we need to reevaluate the tools we've been using and perhaps our entire approach.

There have been lots of tools offered to pastors and church leaders for fixing their churches through the years. In fact, it seems as if we've been spectators at a *parade of solutions* designed to solve the problems that afflict the local church.

This "parade" began about 30 years ago, when what was called the "Church Growth movement" beckoned us to hop on their bandwagon leading the parade. Many of us climbed aboard. Then came a dynamic Drum Major twirling his baton and announcing that our churches needed a vision, lest we perish (like the proverbial *Frog in The Kettle*). Following him came the beauty queens, with their sashes and glittering tiaras. Riding along in gleaming convertibles, they carried signs encouraging us to make our services more seeker friendly and "culturally attractive."

Other floats paraded past, smaller, but just as compelling: One promoted cell groups, another church planting, still another elder-led vs. congregationally-led church governments. Then came the marching bands trumpeting big churches, big worship, and big personalities. Toward the end of the parade, the whole entourage decided to go multi-site and take the spectacle to other communities.

Finally, we hear a fire engine's siren signaling the end of the parade. However, a banner draped across the truck's back end calls us to consider afresh the importance of discipleship. We have been catalyzed, missionalized, and mesmerized by this dynamic parade of programs, all designed to "fix" the local church and make it better!

Can biblical backing be found for the programs we've seen come and go? No doubt. So, what's the problem? First, we have to ponder how much of this "fix it" mentality flows from our culture. American individualism, entrepreneurism, and pragmatism often gets vigorously applied to the church as if it were purely a business organization rather than a spiritual organism. This dangerous cultural practice is often at odds with the eternal results we seek. Maybe instead of us trying to "fix" the Bride, we need to ask the Groom to *heal* us instead!

Second, we may have actually been trying to "fix" the wrong things and in the wrong way, like nailing a board to a broken leg or sandblasting a ruptured appendix. In churches where underlying spiritual and relational diseases exist, it is unrealistic to expect God to bless our programs geared to fix things when we need a Great Physician to *heal* them supernaturally. No amount of programmatic change will heal the systemic health problems that many churches carry.

Systemic corporate pain has less to do with *our activities and programs* and more to do with *who we are and who we have been historically.* Indicators of how well a church functions on a systemic level include healthy communication, spiritual growth and reproduction, trust in leadership, and whether a church's overall spirit is joyful or not. Interactions in these areas make up the process of healthy living in community. If things on a process level are not healthy, all the structural, organizational or programmatic changes we implement will fall short of "fixing" anything. In effect, our unhealthy *ways of relating* within the body hinder the Holy Spirit's ability to produce the ministry fruit we long to see.

The Israelites in Haggai's day faced a problem with their "ways" too. They were taken up with decorating their homes while the temple lay in ruins. Haggai challenged God's people to *consider their ways.* The Israelites couldn't understand why it seemed their purses had "holes" in them, why their economy limped along. They couldn't grasp why their food supplies ran short. Not until Haggai started preaching, did the Israelites begin to understand that they needed solutions to *systemic problems* (problems that affected the Israelites as a group). Their leaders had not been asking the right questions about these symptoms. Haggai explains that they will experience God's blessing only *after* they address their underlying problems (self-interest, apathy, wrong priorities, and the resulting dilapidated condition of God's house). No matter what programmatic steps they took to fix their economy or the famine, their frustration and poverty continued until they finally took the right approach, which included responding to God's Word directly. The purpose of this book is to help you discern if *your* church's "ways" are healthy or not, and if they need corrective, *healing* actions to remove the hindrances to your ministry.

SYSTEMIC HEALTH & LOCAL CHURCHES

How does a *systemic* perspective differ from programmatic approaches and the kind of problem-solving most church leaders do as they sit in Board or Staff meetings? An illustration might help. At the stadium where our family goes to watch our favorite professional baseball team, the between-inning antics often get everyone's attention. One crowd favorite is the Home Depot Tool Race. It involves four people dressed as oversized tools; consisting of a supersized paintbrush, a drill, a hammer, and a bucket. They race around the warning track. It is never a "clean race." The paintbrush tries to trip the hammer or the drill bumps off the bucket. One or two of the tools almost always ends up on the ground and never make it to the finish line. And as this tool race has been going on for years now, the original four people have been replaced by new ones, but the behavior has stayed exactly the same!

The tools in the tool race could just as well represent the problem-solving methods we use in leadership, one bumping out another as we try to "solve the problems" we see. We fire, hire, split, replace, reorganize, etc. to find healthy functioning. But when we minister beside each other, the same unhealthy things keep happening.

Systemic health has more to do with *how* the race is run and *why* we run it this way. It looks at how the "tools" have been relating to each other, and possibly doing so for years. Do they communicate in healthy ways as they travel down the track? Do they sabotage or injure each other along the way? Does the drill have a history of bad behavior toward the paintbrush? Why does the bucket constantly get in the way? How come the hammer acts so heavy handed? Why do the other tools put up with the hammer's big head? And how come the paintbrush always tries to cover things up?

Such unhealthy relational patterns in the family of God can have long-term spiritual implications. Just as in a physical body, when our systemic health is poor, God has designed our bodies to "let us know" through pain and weakness. Christ—the Lord of our church—uses pain and weakness to get our attention in our church the same way. He uses corporate painful symptoms to signal us that something is not right. But until we realize the true spiritual cause and purpose of the pain, we keep running in our dysfunctional tool race. And, unaddressed, sometimes the pain grows great enough to cause complete ministry failure.

For example, the Israelites in Haggai's day had a penchant for ignoring God's house in favor of fixing up their private homes. This led God to bring pain into their lives. God sends pain in the form of a bad economy and famine, to draw attention to their underlying ill health *as a group*. In many churches and denominations, (not to mention the nation) God is doing the same thing today. He sees our poor systemic health and tries to get our attention about it by sending various means of corporate pain. In the meantime, until we realize what's going on, we function much like the tool race at the stadium. We keep bumping into each other and stumble along in our misguided assessment of our situation.

REVIEW

In this section we began to differentiate between "church growth" teaching and "systemic health." The former tends toward a programmatic orientation, the latter toward relational and spiritual dynamics in the body. We noted that the Lord actively seeks to bring systemic problems to the attention of church leaders. He does this through painful events in the life of a church that signal and flow from deeper unresolved problems.

CHAPTER 2

The Biblical Roots of Church Growth/Church Health Teaching

Both church growth principles, (more commonly referred to today as "church health") and the principles related to a church's "systemic health" have biblical roots. Let's focus first on current church health programs. Most current church health teaching consists of ten principles that derive mainly from the early chapters of the Book of Acts.

What are the ten principles common to most church health programs? And how do they relate to the early church in the book of Acts? While it may seem old hat to some readers, a *brief* description of each will help us later when we differentiate the principles of church health from a church's systemic health. (See Figure 1)

1. Multiplying Qualified Leaders – All church health programs recognize the need to find, train and multiply qualified leaders. The early church did too. One of Peter's first actions focused on finding a qualified replacement for Judas Iscariot, who betrayed Christ (Acts 1:15-26). Even in the church's infancy, qualifications emerged for fulfilling the role of an apostle. Peter laid out the requirement for candidates as having "accompanied us all the time that the Lord Jesus went in and out among us, beginning with the baptism of John until the day that He was taken up from us . . ." You sense the faithfulness they sought in Judas' replacement.

Figure 1
The Biblical Roots of Church Growth/Church Health Teaching

Key Principle	Jerusalem Church
Multiplying Qualified Leaders	Acts 1:15-26; 6:1-6
Finding Your Role in Ministry	Acts 6:1-6, 13:1-2
Growing Spirituality	Acts 1:14; 2:42; 4:32
Structural Growth	Acts 6:1-6
Powerful Worship	Acts 2:1-40; 4:23-31
Home Groups	Acts 2:46b; 5:42
Evangelism	Acts 1:8; 2:37-41; 3:11-26; 4: 20; 5:30-32; 6:1; 8:4
Sacrificial, Loving Fellowship	Acts 2:44-45; 4:32, 34-35;
Biblical Theology	Acts 2:42a; 6:2,4
Clear Sense of Purpose	Acts 1:8; 4:12

It was a good thing Peter filled Judas' office. On the day of Pentecost the church would experience explosive growth, a twenty-five fold increase in membership, from 120 to 3000! It would require *many* leaders to disciple all the new converts. Can you imagine? Before Pentecost, the church of 120 in the upper room represented 100% of the Jerusalem church's attendance. After Pentecost, that same 120 would suddenly represent only 4% of the whole congregation! No wonder all church health programs encourage equipping new leaders. The principle supports and often anticipates numerical growth.

2. Finding Your Unique Role in Ministry – Whether under the umbrella of discipleship or gift-oriented ministry, helping people find their unique role in ministry mirrors the biblical pattern. In the early church the apostles knew some of their roles and clarified others as time went on. They felt they should not "neglect the word of God in order to serve tables." However, for the deacons who emerge in Acts 6:1-6, serving the tables of those neglected proved a passion. Other gifted people in roles get identified later in the book of Acts, for example: "Now there were at Antioch, in the church that was there, prophets and teachers . . ." (Acts 13:1). Encouraging the development of spiritual gifts assimilates believers into the life of the church and facilitates the growth of the body, both qualitatively and quantitatively.

3. Growing Spirituality – The church at Ephesus, at the end of the first century, received criticism from Jesus for having "lost its first love." But we see something very different in the in the early days of the Church in Acts 2. The Jerusalem church's devotion to prayer, to the apostles' teaching, to breaking bread together and fellowship, gets recorded for all time (Acts 2:42, 46). They eagerly met together at the temple (large group) and from house to house (small group). One of the amazing things to note relates to how often they met. The Bible tells us they met *every day!* No complacency, no lethargy, no going to church because they felt an obligation. The church health movement, likewise, aims to make church a place people love to be, shaped by each member's love for Jesus.

4. Structural Change – As the Early Church grew, leadership structures needed to change to accommodate growth, which comes out most clearly in the choosing of deacons in Acts 6. The choosing of "the seven" created a new office in the church, a new layer of leadership, and demonstrates that the early Church had a flexible approach to structure, doing what they needed to in order to accommodate their increased numbers and ministry demands. Many authors of major church health programs would agree. Most of them come out of a mega-church experience. You don't become a mega-church without adjusting the organizational structure of the church along the way. New layers of leaders get added as the church grows. It has to! It happened in the early church and happens today in the model offered by current church health programs.

5. Powerful Worship – The worship of the Jerusalem church jumps off the pages of Acts. The crowd's response to Peter's message indicates the powerful impact of their worship. Have you ever sat in a church service where people in the congregation, under the conviction of the Holy Spirit, cried out in response to the Gospel, "Brethren, what shall we do?" (Acts 2:37) All church health programs challenge churches to take a hard look at the quality, purpose, and relevance of their worship. If only such programs could rekindle the inspiration and power we witness in the worship of the Jerusalem church!

6. Home Groups – This often gets connected with "small group ministry" in church health literature. Many New Testament churches met in homes for obvious reasons. We see that pattern begin in Acts 2:46, "breaking bread from house to house." Homes still provide a place for relationships to blossom. They promote hospitality, prayer, discipleship and facilitate evangelism. Today's church health movement also recognizes the importance of home groups. Small groups offer a way to effectively assimilate people into the life of the church.

7. Evangelism – When you survey the early chapters of Acts, you cannot miss the believers' eagerness to share Christ and how God blessed their efforts. The Gospel flowed freely from the lips of disciples into the hearts of hearers. Here are some examples:

> "So then, those who had received his word were baptized; and there were added that day about three thousand souls" (Acts 2:41).

> "And the Lord was adding to their number day by day those who were being saved" (Acts 2:47).

> "But many of those who had heard the message believed, and the number of the men came to be about five thousand" (Acts 4:4).

> "And with great power the apostles were giving witness to the resurrection of the Lord Jesus, and abundant grace was upon them all" (Acts 4:33).

> "And every day, in the temple and from house to house they kept right on teaching and preaching Jesus as the Christ" (Acts 5:42).

> "And the word of God kept on spreading; and the number of the disciples continued to increase greatly in Jerusalem, and a great many of the priests were becoming obedient to the faith" (Acts 6:7).

> "Therefore, those who had been scattered went about preaching the word" (Acts 8:4).

Believers sharing the message of Christ leaps off the pages in Acts. Likewise, all modern church health ministries encourage an enthusiasm for evangelism.

8. Sacrificial, Loving, Fellowship – Acts paints a picture of fellowship that seems different than today's version. In the best case scenario the fellowship we experience today is of the same spirit of what we see in the early church. However, the degree and extent of the early believers' love and sacrifice generally surpasses what we know. "And all those who had believed were together, and had all things in common and they began selling their property and possessions and were sharing them with all, as anyone might have need" (Acts 2:44-45). "And not one of them claimed that anything belonging to him was his own; but all things were common property to them" (Acts 4:32). That's a tough act to follow! Nevertheless, that kind of self-sacrifice is definitely a marker of a vibrant, healthy church.

9. Biblical Theology – Acts 2:42 tells us that the disciples were "devoted to the apostles' teaching." The "*apostles' teaching*" is as sound as theology gets! The apostles "devoted themselves to prayer and the ministry of the word" (Acts 6:4). Their commitment to the ministry of the word drove them to study the scriptures, and they developed a theological framework and an apologetic to guide the new movement. Without sound biblical theology undergirding it, church health principles can embark on a dangerous path that leads to shallow or unstable faith that wavers in times of testing or is easily misled.

10. Clear Sense of Purpose – Every modern church health program would embrace having a clear sense of purpose or mission or vision. However, that purpose might vary among the different programs. One approach might focus on reaching the lost, others focus on worship or teaching or small groups. Part of what makes any ministry model effective rests in a commitment to the mission God lays on the hearts of a church's leaders.

We see a clear sense of purpose in the early church too. Jesus spelled out the early church's purpose in Acts 1:8, "You shall be My witnesses both in Jerusalem, and in all Judea and Samaria, and even to the remotest part of the earth." Peter and the other apostles were committed to fulfilling this mission. When opposition arose, they boldly declared, "We must obey God rather than men" (Acts 5:29). Many paid with their own lives, like Stephen in Acts 7. Giving your life in the pursuit of your mission? Now, that's purpose-driven indeed!

MINISTRY SLIPPAGE

How do we ensure that these ten biblical principles bear fruit in a church's ministry, and how can we explain why they sometimes don't? When churches bear healthy fruit, it is because they are properly linked to the Vine which supports them, and He pours His life into them. The body system He created us to be, linking us together in His Church, operates as He intended. But when we are not properly "linked" to Him because of poor systemic or "bodily" health, then what we call "ministry slippage" occurs. Across the Evangelical landscape today we see *lots* of such slippage. Congregations and their leaders, eager to grow their ministries, overlook their "spiritual medical history" or misdiagnose their symptoms. This prevents church health principles from ever gaining traction.

Implementing church health principles in a *systemically* unhealthy church reminds me of trying to drive up a hill on an icy road. You get *lots* of slippage. Gravity will pull you backwards! And when a car's tires start spinning on the ice, the driver finds that traction, moving forward, and even steering prove dicey. Trying to make progress, you go backwards; and you really don't know where you're going to end up, but it won't be pretty. It's not because you don't know where you *want* to go missionally; it is because the systemic conditions actually *prevent* it. The problem actually is one of traction in a church as well. Systemically unhealthy churches can resist all efforts to get them going, and be hard to handle, even dangerous, to leaders trying to steer the ministry.

Systemic health has to do with the conditions under which your ministry functions. Unlike the conditions in which a car operates on an icy road, a church's "conditions" tend to be *internal and historical*. These conditions can create resistance to progress across an entire ministry. When internal or historical conditions impact the whole "system," we call them "systemic factors." In the same way church health principles derive from Scripture, systemic factors which determine the success or failure of a church's ministry likewise emerge from Scripture. We will cover these in the next chapter.

REVIEW

Most major, published church health programs contain significant similarities to each other in the principles they espouse. The principles are derived from the pages of Scripture, primarily in the Book of Acts. Church health programs teach helpful New Testament concepts. But in churches where the prerequisite underlying "body health" is not evident, deeper work is needed for church health principles to gain traction. When a church attempts to implement church health principles without assessing the nature of the body's systemic health, church leaders often experience a high degree of ministry frustration, not knowing where the resistance to their efforts originates.

If as a result of reading this book you realize your church's systemic health needs treatment, please read *Healing the Heart of Your Church* by Dr. Kenneth Quick **before taking other actions.**

CHAPTER 3

The Biblical Roots of a Church's Systemic Health

Recently, I took our boat out on a new 600 acre reservoir located on the fringe of our county. The lake borders two different scenes. To the East sits a golf course, upscale housing, and a small airport. To the West, the rolling hills of a farm sweep across the landscape. But the farmer has done something curious. From the center of the lake, a boater sees that he built a small chapel in the middle of his property. It's beautiful. Painted brilliant white, it stands out against the backdrop of green fields. The chapel has a simple cross atop a short steeple framed by blue skies. No signage directs you to this church and no public access road exists. Only from the middle of the lake do you even catch a glimpse of it.

Compare that scene to another church I recently visited. On a trip to Savanah, GA, my wife and I took a brief look at St. John the Baptist Catholic church. Open to the public, we went inside for a peek. What a sight! While the exterior sports two soaring towers, the outside of the church gives little hint of what grandeur awaits you within. The scale appears monumental. The main aisle stretches 114 feet and looks much longer. The ceiling hovers seven stories above your head. The interior colors gleam with vibrancy. Over eighty stained glass windows dazzle the eye. From the balcony a gigantic, shining pipe organ reigns like royalty over the sanctuary. The church bell weighs over two tons. All told the church exceeds 28,000 square feet.[5] What an edifice!

---

[5] http://www.savannahcathedral.org/virtual_tour/cathedral_trivia

Churches differ in many ways, not just in size or location. They may be liturgical or spontaneous in worship; they differ theologically; they may be white collar or blue, multi-cultural or homogeneous, rural or urban. Some churches are young and hip while others are old and full of hip replacements! However, when we examine the differences between two particular New Testament churches, we can recognize the biblical roots of systemic dynamics.

For instance, no two New Testament churches differ more than the Jerusalem church as described in Acts and the church at Corinth as described in Paul's epistles. One consisted of Hebraic stock; the other, while birthed out of a Jewish synagogue (Acts 18), contained mostly Gentile converts of pagan background (1 Cor. 12:2).[6] The Jerusalem church displayed a beautiful sense of corporate unity. Their "one mind" gets described *four* times (Acts 1:14; 2:46; 4:32; 5:12). Contrast that with the disunity evident in the church at Corinth, something that appeared to have begun early-on in its existence (1 Corinthians 1:10-17). While speaking in tongues proved a powerful evangelistic witness in the Jerusalem church (Acts 2:5-12), it caused the church at Corinth to nearly come unglued (1 Cor. 12-14). The Jerusalem church continually "devoted themselves to the apostles teaching and to fellowship, and to the breaking of bread" (Acts 2:42). In contrast some Corinthian believers abused communion (1 Cor. 11), others were suing each other in court (1 Cor. 6), and still others caused some believers to stumble over the food they ate (1 Cor. 8).

The Jerusalem saints held the apostles in high esteem while the Corinthian believers scrutinized and unfavorably evaluated Paul's ministry. Finally, the church at Jerusalem fended off an infection of sin that threatened their congregation, in relation to Ananias and Sapphira (Acts 5); while the Corinthian believers failed to deal properly with the sinful behavior of at least one of their members (1

---

[6] D.A. Carson, *Showing the Spirit* (Grand Rapids: Baker, 1987) 26.

Cor. 5).

Comparing these two churches and witnessing the quagmire of the Corinthian church in particular, we get a picture of two kinds of systemic functioning. Churches are *bodies* according to the apostle Paul's metaphor (i.e. a system of systems that works as a collective whole). We can therefore see the issues in the Corinthian church as an example of *systemic dysfunction*. The church at Corinth was marked by so much disunity that the apostle Paul claims they are like "mere men." He uses a body analogy to make his point in 1 Corinthians 12, using bodily systemic functioning and connections to illustrate both the healthy and unhealthy ways believers relate in the local church. He says:

> [12] For even as the body is one and *yet* has many members, and all the members of the body, though they are many, are one body, so also is Christ. [13] For by one Spirit we were all baptized into one body, whether Jews or Greeks, whether slaves or free, and we were all made to drink of one Spirit. [14] For the body is not one member, but many. [15] If the foot says, "Because I am not a hand, I am not *a part* of the body," it is not for this reason any the less *a part* of the body. [16] And if the ear says, "Because I am not an eye, I am not *a part* of the body," it is not for this reason any the less *a part* of the body. [17] If the whole body were an eye, where would the hearing be? If the whole were hearing, where would the sense of smell be? [18] But now God has placed the members, each one of them, in the body, just as He desired. [19] If they were all one member, where would the body be? [20] But now there are many members, but one body. [21] And the eye cannot say to the hand, "I have no need of you"; or again the head to the feet, "I have no need of you." [22] On the contrary, it is much truer that the members of the body which seem to be weaker are

necessary; [23] and those *members* of the body which we deem less honorable, on these we bestow more abundant honor, and our less presentable members become much more presentable, [24] whereas our more presentable members have no need *of it*. But God has *so* composed the body, giving more abundant honor to that *member* which lacked, [25] so that there may be no division in the body, but *that* the members may have the same care for one another. [26] And if one member suffers, all the members suffer with it; if *one* member is honored, all the members rejoice with it.

The apostle works hard to get the divided Corinthian church reunited. His body analogy enables us to see beyond the programs which often dominate church life and delve instead into how the church operates as a living spiritual organism. Without stretching Paul's analogy too far, or deviating from his main point, we can identify the defining characteristic of the church's systemic nature: *We are profoundly and eternally connected to each other, and the way we understand, value, and treat each other has serious ramifications.*

To state the obvious, in Paul's body analogy, *a fundamental interrelationship exists between the parts of the body and the body as a whole.* He puts it this way: "For even as the body is one and *yet* has many members, and all the members of the body, though they are many, are one body, so also is Christ." (vs. 12). Once we come to Christ through the Spirit, whatever our ethnicity or station in life, we become members of the larger Body of Christ.

What does that mean for the health of your church? It means that, because of our union with each other and with Christ, what happens to one part of the body impacts the *whole*. This dynamic becomes apparent when the sad news of a church leader's moral failure gets announced from a pulpit. A sudden gasp of shock hits the congregation *in unison*. And after the shock, the congregation begins to feel the pain of his action *as a group*. We *collectively* experience the heartbreak Christ himself must feel over such a tragedy.

I have witnessed a different collective reaction at the wedding of a much loved young couple. These two sweet people worked hard to honor Christ in their lives before their marriage. At the end of the wedding ceremony, when they were announced as husband and wife, spontaneous and enthusiastic applause broke out. We all rejoiced *as one*, at the good news. These illustrations speak to the interconnectedness of the Body of Christ. Paul's words at the end of his body analogy spell it out, "And if one member suffers, all the members suffer with it; if *one* member is honored, all the members rejoice with it" (vs. 26).

OTHER REFERENCES

Paul also uses this body analogy in his letters to the Romans, Ephesians, and Colossians. In Romans 12:4-5 he writes, "For just as we have many members in one body and all the members do not have the same function, so we, who are many, are one body in Christ, *and individually members one of another* (italics mine). The nature of our vital union in the Body of Christ extends not only to our connection with the body as a whole, but with the other members too. When conflict enters a church, it is never the hands vs. the feet, or the eyes vs. the ears. In the unique mystical union, found only in the church, the hands are as much a part of the feet as the feet are a part of the hands. The eyes work in relationship with the ears. If you think about it, the eyes and ears have a very close working relationship (i.e. if you hear a loud noise in another part of your house and immediately turn your head to *see* what it's about!) No body part functions in complete isolation. The body works as a unit, made of mutually dependent parts. The body only functions as a unit, in a *healthy* way, when the parts work together. God designed them to do so, and they cannot escape their identification with the body. As such, when conflicts come into the local church, it is never the nose vs. the toes as separate entities. The parts of the body cannot escape their identification with other parts of the same body. Because of our membership *in* one another, no one escapes pain when the body suffers disunity or some other trauma. Likewise when something good happens in one part of the body, the whole church should rejoice. Why? Because of the tightly integrated nature of our membership with one another in the Body of Christ.

In Ephesians 4:15-16 Paul writes, "but speaking the truth in love, we are to grow up in all *aspects* into Him who is the head, *even* Christ, from whom the whole body, being fitted and held together by what every joint supplies, according to the proper working of each individual part, causes the growth of the body for the building up of itself in love." In systemic health, we look at how individual parts of the body relate to each other, not just how healthy they are as an individual "body part." Take the bones of your wrist for example. The surfaces of the bones in your wrist are relatively flat, allowing your hand to move in multiple directions. At the point where the wrist and forearm bone-heads meet, a special lubricant called synovial fluid reduces friction and keeps the bones moving freely. Problems with synovial fluid lead to joint *pain*. I like how Eph. 4:15 starts, "but speaking the truth in love" and vs. 16 ends, "for the building up of itself in love," because it illustrates how love *lubricates* joints in the body of Christ, and keeps them operating smoothly. You could say that the Corinthian congregation needed such extra lubricant to lessen friction between some of their bone-heads! We're not much different today.

The way believers are wired together in the Body of Christ is so organic that Paul could warn the church at Corinth, "a little leaven leavens the whole lump of dough" (1 Cor. 5:6). The backdrop of his warning related to the ongoing attitude of pride of the

Corinthian believers over the immoral man in their congregation, leading to their failure to address it righteously. Paul sees that, without corrective measures, the church's entire culture could become infected. By failing to address sin in the body, confusion about appropriate behavior can become contagious. It would spread through the relational and spiritual network that binds the body together. We see this happen all the time!

Jesus values the relational and spiritual network in the local church highly. Matthew 5:23-24 reveals that reconciled relationships are more important than whatever offering we might have to give Him. "Therefore if you are presenting your offering at the altar, and there remember that your brother has something against you, leave your offering there before the altar and go; first be reconciled to your brother, and then come and present your offering." If they followed this principle of "reconciliation before offering" in the church at Corinth as it existed when Paul wrote his letter their budget would be in the red. The congregation was so divided that few offerings would have been considered acceptable. Imagine what would happen if we strictly held to that standard in our churches today. Put nothing in the offering plate if you have a brother or sister with whom you are unreconciled!

In observations drawn from our consulting work with churches, we find that Jesus does not overlook the "reconciliation-before-offering" principle, even if we do. He commonly brings *financial pain* into churches where underlying relational problems exist. He does this to draw attention to systemic problems church leaders have ignored. Unfortunately church leaders often misinterpret the spiritual significance of these things. We still give our offerings, but in churches where corporate dysfunction occurs, the offerings often fail to meet the current needs. When we give in spite of Jesus' admonition to fix relational problems first, He has ways of making it seem as if we never gave in the first place! His word will not return void, even though our offerings might.

DEEPER DYNAMICS

The systemic approach to church health affirms that our interconnectedness with each other impacts the quality of all the things that the church health/church growth movement trumpets: fellowship, ministry training, the authenticity of our message and our evangelism, the vibrancy of our worship, the effectiveness of our prayers, and the success of our mission. Every behavior highlighted by those who teach church growth or church health principles gets impacted by the underlying systemic health of a local church.

We start to see how systemic health differs from the various programs we employ to grow our church's ministry and how it relates to traction for those things we seek to do. Systemic functioning deals with the internal dynamics of a church. Church health/church growth focuses mainly on external manifestations of church life—i.e. our *programs*. Systemic health focuses on how we *relate* to each other and to God corporately. A church can do lots of things together and keep a lot of programs running while it is systemically sick. Of the unhealthy churches with which we have consulted, all met for worship, all prayed, all participated in missions, all ate meals together, all promoted small groups, and all made attempts at evangelism. They had the *marks* of "healthy" churches, yet were far from it. What was wrong? In most cases, church leaders sought to resolve systemic problems with *programmatic* solutions. That's how their business, military or management training taught them to do it. While the activities of an unhealthy church may resemble the activities of a healthy church, the unhealthy church's activities get undermined by poor spiritual and relational functioning. The body manifests "corporate sickness."

In reality, your church represents Christ on earth as His Body. That was His intent. Because of the church's unique nature, not only is the quality of church life impacted by how we relate to each other, but Jesus takes an ongoing active interest in the condition of each local church on the planet.

1 Corinthians 11 reveals how He paid attention to the division in that church. The Corinthian believers ignored their divisions and partook of the Lord's Supper as if nothing were the matter. Paul tells them they failed "to discern the body rightly." As a result, he explains, "For this reason many among you are weak and sick, and a number sleep" (1 Cor. 11:30). Is Paul addressing those who have a tendency, like Eutychus, to fall asleep during his messages? No, what Paul describes concerns churches that have so ignored their systemic bodily health that the Lord Himself steps in to address it with physical symptoms! "Sleep," functions as a euphemism for physical death. We know that some chronic illness can result in physical sickness and even death, but the cause in the case of the Corinthians finds its root, not in the natural result of aging, but in highly symbolic supernatural intervention and chastisement.

Our union in Christ's body bears real meaning to Jesus. He sees the true state of a local church's internal health. Being born again into His body, each of us has a role to play which contributes to its health. He chooses our gifts and assigns our calling, but we often fail to realize that how we fulfill our ministry role in relation to others in the body carries serious spiritual repercussions.

To summarize, today's church health principles focus mostly on *external* issues that are programmatic. They include things like leadership development, organization, staffing, attraction methods, assimilation, small groups, and future-oriented strategic plans. These elements largely consist of a church's outward face. A church's systemic health, on the other hand, involves deeper dynamics that determine how well a church is functioning *as a body*. It includes spiritual and relational undercurrents that shape the way people connect to their Lord and each other as they seek to fulfill what He has called them to do.

Systemic health reflects a church's spirit and quality of interpersonal functioning. It is a function of abiding in Christ *corporately*. It reflects His Life flowing in us and between us. Without that Life expressed systemically, and the nature of the love it produces in us and between us, we quickly start to operate as "mere men."

Do internal and external aspects of church life overlap? Certainly. However, many church leaders emphasize externals and programmatic activities that do not ask or deal with whether the church is actually able to do these things in a healthy way. This is where many churches have actually believed a lie: Do the right things and you will grow and be healthy. Jesus taught clearly in John 15 that success in fruit-bearing, the "doing" of ministry, is totally dependent on the vibrancy of the connection of the branches with the Vine, and, one might assume, the branches and each other, as they/we are *all* interconnected.

Forgive me for sounding repetitive, but, when we ignore systemic spiritual health in a congregation, and seek to implement church growth/church health principles, we will not find fruit-bearing comes easily. Many churches today languish, not because they haven't sought to implement programs encouraged by church health seminars and books, but because they overlook the quality of their church's systemic functioning, whether they are actually a *healthy body*. In the next section we will examine five key areas to systemic health with which you can quickly assess in your ministry.

REVIEW

In this section we've attempted to show, that while churches may differ in many ways, they all share a systemic nature. The systemic nature of the local church is illustrated by Paul's body analogy, which he uses in several New Testament passages. The church's systemic nature is founded on the biblical fact that a spiritual union binds believers together relationally before God in the local assembly. Jesus monitors the quality of each church's spiritual life, sometimes intervening through the use of corporate chastisement to correct problems He sees. Finally, we saw that systemic health relates to deeper dynamics that reveal how well a church body functions.

CHAPTER 4

The Five Spheres of a Church's Systemic Health

The town I grew up in featured an old Woolworth's store. It had a front and rear entrance that provided a short cut between my house and the town square. As a kid, I took that shortcut often. Whenever I did, I had to walk past a dining area where you could sit down and order a burger or a banana split. Across from the main counter was a large dart board with balloons attached to it. Each balloon contained a piece of paper offering a discount on the cost of a banana split. If you were going to order one, they handed you a dart. You would throw the dart, pop a balloon, and see if you hit that special balloon containing a slip of paper that read "free banana split." That's a fun memory, but I doubt throwing darts in a department store will ever come back into vogue. Can you imagine giving customers today a sharp projectile and telling them to throw it? Who knows where it would end up!

Churches with poor systemic health usually suffer from problems in five "spheres" of church life. Each sphere contains a message, much like those balloons at Woolworth's. These five spheres either tell the story of the joy of church life when things are healthy or the pain and turmoil of ministry when they are not. What is crucial to realize is that, when problems show up in one area, because they are interconnected (systemic), it multiplies the potential for problems to spread into the other areas. As a result it should not surprise you to find that a church with painful issues in one "sphere" will often have them in several others as well.

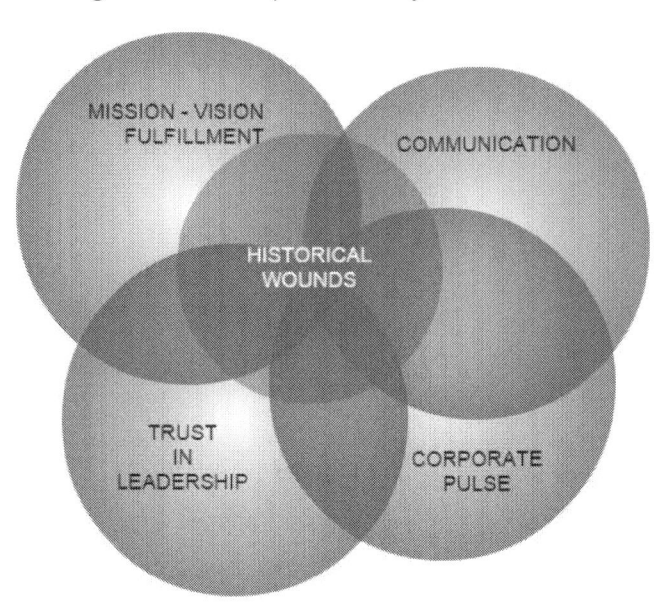

Figure 2 – Five Spheres of Systemic Health

- MISSION - VISION FULFILLMENT
- COMMUNICATION
- HISTORICAL WOUNDS
- TRUST IN LEADERSHIP
- CORPORATE PULSE

THE INTERRELATED NATURE OF SYSTEMS

I know a family whose house was recently struck by lightning. They were at church on a Sunday morning when it happened. They returned home to discover that everything related to their home's electrical system was fried. Their HVAC, computers, and television - all destroyed. If it was connected to an electrical socket – it got wrecked. Did you know that most of the electrical sockets and switches in the average home are "daisy chained" together? That means the wires travel from one outlet or switch to another. Unless you have an outlet on a dedicated circuit, most of the outlets are wired together in groups and labeled accordingly in your electrical panel. If a problem occurs in one area of the house you can often fix it by resetting that circuit. However when some internal or external force impacts the entirety of your system, you can have a much bigger problem.

We see the same thing on even a larger scale when you have a "black-out," an electrical outage that occurs across a region of the country. The "great blackouts" of 1965, 1977 and 2003 all caused widespread damage throughout the Northeast because the nation's electrical grid is connected one to the other. And when the grid goes down, it impacts every house, business, and street light tied to it. The cause for the blackout could be as obscure as trees rubbing against power lines in a remote part of the system or due to squirrels shorting out the lines! The causes vary, but the results are widespread because it is an *interrelated* system.

The church doesn't operate on wires and electrical impulses, but it is no less interconnected. Its conductors are relationships, its voltage the power of the Holy Spirit. It's not hard to see how God's work gets short-circuited when relational wounds or broken trust in leadership are unhealed within a local church body. In our consulting ministry we have come to see such corporate wounds as Satan's primary means for derailing a church's ministry. Ministry should never be primarily about human effort, but about the life of Jesus manifested in the midst of His people as they gather in His name. If people have been wounded somehow in a church, and nothing has been done to help the body heal, it compromises the relational network of the local body and discharges the Spirit's power - weakening its impact.

There is a modern tendency to focus on the *activities* of the early church and model current programs on their *behaviors*. But that says nothing about the history of the church or potential damaged spiritual or relational dynamics. We forget how freely the Holy Spirit was moving in the Jerusalem church, how He was filling the leaders and the people, all of which lubricated the "activities" of Acts 2:42. In trying to replicate the early church, it's possible to copy these activities while neglecting the filling and flow of the Holy Spirit Who animated them at the beginning.

When we do so we are left with skeletal programs which we try to run mechanically, not requiring the Spirit's energizing dynamic within the Body. We end up going through the motions of running these programs, wondering why we don't see what they saw in the First Century. In effect, we rob the process of its supernatural empowerment. Again how does this happen? It happens because we overlook the interrelated nature of the body Christ has created us to be.

We may overlook it, but God does not. He waits for us to discern our bodily illness and/or weakness and then to take steps to heal it and to reconcile with those who may be wounded before His Spirit will bless our ministries with the kind of supernatural impact we long for and which our world desperately needs to see from the Church at large.

ILLUSTRATION FROM AGRIGCULTURE

At a conference where I spoke, I explained the systemic nature and interconnectedness of the local church. Afterwards one of the attendees enlightened me about the use of what he called "systemic pesticides" in farming. "Systemic pesticides" illustrate how a church's systemic functioning can work for good or ill. It turns out that, if a pesticide is soluble in water, the chemicals can be placed in the ground and will migrate up the plant's root system and throughout the plant, which makes the *entire plant* toxic to invaders. Bug eats plant; bug dies.

However, this method (obviously) only works on plants which are *not* meant for human consumption. Just as the plant's system of roots absorb chemicals that spread throughout the entire plant, so health or poison will spread through the interconnected spiritual and emotional relationships in the local church. When poison makes its way into the body of Christ, it will make the whole body toxic over time. However, this same interconnectedness can result in the spread of health too. When a church addresses the issues which have made it toxic and draws from the resurrection life-force Jesus provides, that new life will spread through the same relational system and supernatural spiritual fruit begins to appear again.

THE FAMILY AS A SYSTEM

The place where we are most conscious of the "interconnectedness" is the family. God has created the family to be the place where we learn roles and how to relate to others in general, and to authority in particular. We learn about conflict and how to resolve it (or not), about how love looks and acts, about stewardship and encouragement. We learn it all in the schoolhouse of family. The interconnected system that makes up the family can flow with either health or sickness or a mix of both.

When one family member relates in an unhealthy manner, it will impact how the family functions as a whole, how it has to expend its energy to solve or resolve the unhealthy operation. If the family inappropriately tolerates one member's acting out, enabling the behavior to continue, the dysfunction will start to impact everyone. On the other hand, if one person in the family commits to act in healthier ways, that too will spread through the entire family system positively.

The church is also a big family. It can carry wounds and hurts which members have inflicted on each other just as human families do. And, just like in a family, church problems show up in the same relational areas.

Communication can break down or become reactive. Our *trust in leadership/authority* gets broken when parental or pastoral figures fail us. Dysfunctional leadership in the family or church can create discouragement and suspicion. People start to lose hope that anything will ever change. With leadership in crisis, a church will struggle with *mission/vision fulfillment*. Leaders get resisted as they attempt to implement changes to achieve the mission.

Families and church bodies can both "become depressed," resulting in a weak *corporate pulse or spirit*. Often the source of systemic ills flows from *historical wounds* that sit unhealed, unreconciled. God does not forget these though most churches try hard to do so, and they continue to spin out poison into the body. Relational wounds of one sort or another are usually the source of a family's dysfunction as people react or try to protect themselves by controlling their environment. We often overlook that the same is true of churches!

We now want to turn our attention to these five spheres. It is as I unpack these five interconnected areas of church life that you may begin to recognize how they have become a source of pain in your church community.

CHAPTER 5

Sphere One - The Corporate Pulse

Atrial Fibrillation, or AFib, is a common affliction, one with which I occasionally suffer. I can tell you that, when it strikes, it *completely* unnerves you. You suffer a loss of strength, experience high anxiety, and feel every mistimed "thump" in your chest. You can try every trick you can think of to snap your heart back to a normal rhythm, but they seldom work. While hoping and praying that your heart corrects its pace, you also sometimes wonder if it might be your last day on earth. Your emotions can get out of whack and supersede your faith in such a moment of crisis. The problem of AFib resides, not in the arteries of the heart, but in the body's "electrical system" that fires each beat of your heart. Even with medication you still have to wait and pray to see if that most vital organ will right its rhythm.

A church's "corporate pulse" is the atmosphere or "spirit" or life energy that inhabits a congregation that gathers in Jesus' name. What should be a vibrant atmosphere because of the presence of Christ and the work of His Spirit can likewise get out of rhythm. Instead of the literal beat of normal, healthy church life, a church's corporate pulse can deteriorate, grow weak, and/or become irregular.

Again I'm not talking about the Holy Spirit, but the collective attitude or demeanor or vibrancy of the congregation. This "spirit" often gets associated with Sunday morning worship services, but in reality it permeates every aspect of church life from congregational and board meetings to the choir to what people sense when they walk in the doors of the church.

This is not the same as a church's *style*. Churches seek to create a positive worship "atmosphere" through things like their music, their dress code and their friendliness. In larger churches, stage lights and video productions from teams operating vast sound boards help set this "mood." Some churches install full service coffee bars and caffeinate the congregation into vibrancy. But such stylings are more like decorative elements than what makes up a church's true "spirit" and defines its pulse of life. Modern embellishments may make meeting together more comfortable and relevant, but they do not define a church's actual heartbeat.

Nor is it your church's activities which define its corporate pulse. The pulse *impacts* the activities of your church, but the programs and activities are often the fruit of the pulse of a church. Like the church in Sardis described in Revelation 3:1-6, a church can have tons of activities and programs, and have a reputation that they are alive, but Jesus says that *they have no pulse*: "You have a reputation that you are alive, but you are dead." Two churches may have very similar sets of activities and one be operating with a strong pulse, and the other with no pulse at all.

The church at Sardis had something happen to the pulse of their church. It is clear that pulse had been strong at some point, and the fact that Jesus speaks to it means that believers still inhabit its pews, but *corporately* something happened. It may have happened in your church too. They had all the activities of church going on, but there was no longer any spiritual life or vibrancy about it.

And Jesus *deals* with such churches; He does not just let them die. He tells the believers in Sardis that if the church doesn't listen to Him and fails to respond and change, He will come to them "like a thief," and take away what little life they had left.

Meanwhile, just down the road in Philadelphia (Rev. 3:7-13) we find in contrast an active church with a strong pulse. Jesus said an "open door" for new ministry initiatives and mission had been placed before them. What specifically made these two congregations different? What could a consultant or a District Supervisor in a denomination discern about the two churches and define as the distinction between them? They displayed a different corporate pulse, one that honored the Lord in spite of severe testing and one revved up its activities and lived on its reputation for being a "great church." How many churches fail to distinguish between the activities they pursue and the spiritual pulse with which they pursue them because they equate the two?

This I believe is a mistake many church leaders make when applying the principles of the church health movement. When examining the Jerusalem church in Acts 2:42-47, they focus on the *activities* displayed in their early church life. But the key is not the activities, but the *spirit* that animated those activities. The following chart illustrates the difference between them:

Figure 3: Activities - Pulse Comparison	
Activities of Jerusalem Church	Spirit/Pulse of Jerusalem Church
Teaching	Awe
Fellowship	Selflessness
Communion	Gladness
Prayer	Sincerity of heart
God things – through apostles	Unity
Acts of Sacrifice and Generosity	Praise
Large group meetings	Enjoyed favor with all the people
Home groups	The Lord was adding daily those
Ate together	who were being saved.
Shared Christ	

Why have we become so enamored with the activities of the Jerusalem church? It is because we can *control* them. We cannot make *any* of the things on the right side of the list happen. The church at Jerusalem behaved in ways quite similar to our modern day churches. They received teaching from church leaders, they fellowshipped, took communion, and prayed together. They met in large groups and small. They shared Christ and gave financially to help others. They witnessed "God things" from time to time, experiencing supernatural healings and answers to prayer. But these activities were not its pulse.

We often overlook the descriptors of the pulse here. If church leaders had to weigh which was more important, more necessary, to a healthy church, they'd probably admit that the programs and activities don't count for much unless animated by the kind of underlying spirit the Jerusalem church displayed.

Joy was in the atmosphere. Leaders served willingly and sacrificially. The church enjoyed genuine unity. They demonstrated selflessness, gladness, and sincerity of heart. They found favor with the community around their church, their attitudes being appreciated by a watching world. It was the kind of spirit through which God could pour His blessings and He added people to the body *daily!* If you attended a church like that, you also would be in awe of what God was doing.

Now, do most modern evangelical churches exhibit the *behaviors* and *activities* and *programs* of the early church? For the most part, yes they do. Do they exhibit the *spirit* and *pulse* of the early church? That's the point of this chapter. Church leaders need to be honest about this thing which they cannot control, but which is the actual evidence of Christ abiding in their midst and manifesting His Presence and doing His work when they gather. He is their heartbeat. An accurate reading of your church's pulse is based on how well it reflects this *spirit* of the Jerusalem church, a much better measure of its actual health than the activities of Acts 2:42. So, honestly, how healthy is the beat of your church's corporate heart?

PICK A CHURCH, ANY CHURCH

Consider the following scenario: You are new to a neighborhood and need to find a church home. You decide to visit two outwardly similar churches based on their programs and your family's need. You pull into the church parking lot of the first church on your list. You get out of your car and enter the building. If you are female, it's likely you immediately sense the spirit of the place. You can't help doing so, it's almost involuntary, a part of the equipment God has built into the feminine heart and through which His Spirit now works. You might find the church's spirit positive and joyous, or depressed and heavy. If you are male, this level of discernment often takes a while (months or sometimes years). However, a wise husband will learn to listen to whatever his wife's antennae pick up.

What you are discerning before you get very far in the door is that "pulse." Sometimes something occurred in the church's history—recent or distant—to give it the atmosphere you encounter. If the spirit of the church is warm, gracious, excited and inviting, it is likely that the church's leaders have courageously protected and fostered the health of the church. They have listened to and responded to Jesus' leadership as Lord of their church in past days and He is pleased to show up when they meet and bless their efforts.

But if you walk in and the atmosphere proves stifling, stiff, and sparkless, something has gone terribly wrong along the way. You may not know what, but something has occurred historically on a spiritual and relational plane which has displeased the Lord of the church and limited His willingness to bless the ministry. Churches invariably bury this stuff or justify their actions, but either way the One Whose Presence is required for a vibrant pulse has pulled back, and the church is left with activities but without the energizing

Presence of Christ.

Paul brought up this issue with the Galatians. Their Christian community became diseased through bad theology. The church got infected with false teaching which sought to bring members back under the legalistic yoke of the Old Covenant. The effect of this legalism on their congregation clearly impacted the pulse of the church. Paul asks them, "Where then is that sense of blessing you had? (Gal. 4:15). Another translation puts it: "What has happened to all your joy?"[7] It's a question we at Blessing Point Ministries ask of churches when we consult with them. Something happened among the Galatian believers that changed the pulse of their church. In this case, it was false teaching which led to estrangement from the apostle Paul.

Things happen in our churches to give them irregular heartbeats too, but leaders rarely stop to pay it any mind. We start living with a slower or irregular corporate pulse and that becomes our "new normal," though the church's activities rarely wane. I know a pastor who regularly leads lost people to Christ, but then he instructs them *not* to attend his church! He knows the spirit of his present church would prove dangerous to the health of a baby Christian. Some of you reading this (sadly) would resonate with that pastor!

A church's corporate pulse can get out of rhythm or grow weak for a number of reasons, some of which we explore later in the section on historical wounds. But in general, it suggests unresolved corporate (body) problems beneath the surface of church life, just like it does in a human body. Any doctor diagnosing AFib would know that there are *causes* of which the AFib is only a *symptom*, whether stress or genetics or something else. In a church, a "pulse problem" is similar, often the lingering effects of some corporate crisis that sits unresolved and unreconciled.

---

[7] New International Version

SPHERE ONE – THE CORPORATE PULSE

Paul gives a hint of such a cause among the Corinthians which contributed to their many problems. He says in 1 Cor.12:17, "If the whole body were an eye, where would the hearing be? If the whole were hearing, where would the sense of smell be?" Sometimes one body "part" deems itself so large that it dominates the rest of the body, particularly on a leadership level. If that "part" always gets their way, the spirit of the leadership suffers and the pulse becomes irregular because God did not make the body to be just one "sense" like sight or hearing, or dominated by the operation of one person's gifts. If it should happen (as it regularly does in churches), the rest of the gifted people can begin to feel oppressed or believe that their gift(s) are unimportant. This results in a more sluggish corporate pulse.

In a healthy body, all the parts keep each other in balance and know when to function, preventing the whole body from becoming an ear or an eye. To the extent leaders stay humble and don't try to control or dominate everything and everyone for the sake of their agendas or assume *their* gift is the only gift or the most important gift, the spirit and corporate pulse of your church remains strong.

Modern medicine has developed ways to re-adjust a person's irregular heartbeat back to its normal rhythm. I can tell you from personal experience, that, after an episode of AFib, when your heart finally finds its right rhythm again, you *immediately* feel better. You shift from weakness to strength, from fear to relief, and from obsessing about your condition to getting back to normal life.

There are ways to restore a church's corporate pulse to a healthy rhythm too, with similar dramatic results. No more pushing, shoving, or managing ministry into existence, no more leadership domination or controlling behaviors, no more programs and activities with the hope that God might show up and bless them. The experiences of awe, worship, unity, etc. found in Acts 2 drive the activities of Acts 2:42. In your church it becomes a new vibe that allows you to pursue church related activities with a sense of hope and blessing.

REVIEW

As you reflect on the pulse of your church, ask the Lord to help you discern what drives your church's heartbeat and fuels your church's ministries. Does the resurrection life and Presence of the Lord Jesus animate its ministries and activities? Christ *is* our life (Col.3:4). Be honest to assess how closely your church reflects the *spirit* (not the activities) of the Jerusalem church in the book of Acts. Is the pulse of your ministry strong, or erratic and weak?

Prayerfully consider the following questions that are a part of Blessing Point's ChurchScan Inventory. They can help you determine if your church's activities are fueled by the kind of spirit God can bless.

- Is joy in the atmosphere when your church gathers together?
- Do your church leaders (pastoral, staff and lay leaders) enjoy unity and love among themselves?
- Does God call young people into His service from your church?
- Does your church regularly see conversions from your services and individual evangelism?
- Do pastors at your church feel respected and enjoy long, positive tenures?

CHAPTER 6

<u>Sphere Two - Trust in Leadership</u>

Have you ever been hurt by someone you trusted, maybe a parental figure let you down or perhaps you felt betrayed by someone you thought was your friend? Those in ministry rarely escape such hurt. I often think of God's call of Ezekiel to ministry. God told him that he would feel the sting of scorpions and the stabbing pain of thorns as he carried out what God called him to do. Ezekiel was no missionary to Midian or Assyria; his ministry was to his own people, the Israelites themselves!

I experienced my biggest hurt in ministry as a young church planter. Starting our new church meant relocating one thousand miles, but we happily and excitedly did so! The project received approval by the church planting director for the denomination with which I served. Prayer and financial support for the effort were raised in record time. I moved my family to the town we targeted. We put down roots, got involved in the community, and gathered a small group of new and nonbelievers.

But then something happened to change *everything*. The church planting director resigned about a year into the project. Suddenly, it seemed all he initiated came under scrutiny, including our project. Nothing about what we were doing satisfied the higher ups, though our plan had been reviewed and approved before we started. Here's how the trouble manifested itself: We would make a decision on site, only to have it reversed by church leaders hundreds of miles away uninvolved with the day to day operation. Money designated for our church plant got withheld (for reasons not fully explained). Miscommunication created confusion about the whole project. I concluded that something was very wrong behind the scenes and I was in the dark about it. However, the more I questioned what was happening, the more I became the problem. What a mess! It turned into the most ugly, painful ministry experience of my life. I ended up resigning and limped off into my own personal wilderness, wandering for ten years.

A lack of trust in leadership often finds its roots in stories like mine. Maybe as a pastor you were hurt by an elder or betrayed by a staff member early on in your ministry. Ever since then, you find yourself unable to let down your guard around elders or with staff, even years later serving in a different church. Elders and staff in your current church may never intend to hurt you, but your protective instinct says "You've got to keep your eye on them!"

Sometimes, to protect ourselves, we will encourage a church to change their structure, the pain causing an actual mutation in our ecclesiology. If it was a deacon board that caused you pain, you decide your church needs to be elder-run. Or you decided, after your painful episode with the elder, that you wanted a bylaw that said the pastor should have veto power on any elder nomination. You also asked for the right to interview and choose your staff and want the ability to fire them too.

Or, perhaps you are a lay leader who has faithfully served your church for decades. You have seen pastors come and go through the years, none staying for any great length of time, all seeming to use the church as a stepping stone to a bigger ministry. The potential pain of watching another pastor depart for "greener pastures" leaves you wary about pastors as a whole. You and the board unconsciously protect yourselves by taking on an employer/employee mindset with your next pastoral candidate, seeing them more as a hireling than as a "good shepherd." Viewing a minister in that kind of "business relationship" makes it easier to fire a pastor or to drive him off if he doesn't measure up.

PERSONAL HISTORY AND PUBLIC MINISTRY

Though it seldom gets discussed, our relationship with church authority figures gets further complicated by the history we bring with us into the Body of Christ, and there is often a painful intersection of ministry and personal history. I had to face the fact that some of my alienation from church authority figures was a reflection of my fear and resentment of my parents from my family of origin. That early painful emotional "training" played a role in the dynamics around the excruciating failure of the church plant I mentioned earlier, though years passed before I realized it. Peter Scazzero, in his enlightening book *The Emotionally Healthy Church* (Zondervan, 2003), unpacks that complexity in our relationship with authority figures. He writes, "No matter what kind of ministry you lead, most of the people involved will bring emotional 'baggage' from their families. When you are in a meeting with six other people, there are really many other invisible people present at the table."[8]

Scazzero is right of course, but we bring *more* than just those invisible people with us to the boardroom; we bring the wounds and hurt they've inflicted on us as well. We project the potential for fresh wounding on anyone who fills a role or who talks, looks, or acts like those who perpetrated our pain. Our defenses go up and red flags fly when we encounter such a person. Kenneth Quick writes in *Healing the Heart of Your Church*, "Like the trenches one can still see as remnants of World War I in France, our ancient defenses remain scarring the landscape of our lives long after the painful battles of childhood are over."[9]

---

[8] Peter Scazzero, *The Emotionally Healthy Church* (Grand Rapids: Zondervan, 2003) p. 105.
[9] Kenneth Quick, *Healing the Heart of Your Church* (St. Charles, IL: Churchsmart, 2003) p. 27

We see these family dynamics reflected in the biblical narrative. Moses never quite escapes the anger at a perceived injustice he displays when he kills an Egyptian he finds abusing an Israelite brother. Later in his life, that jumps up to bite him when he strikes the rock at another perceived injustice. It keeps him out of the Promised Land. Try imagining the impact of favoritism in Joseph's family of origin and how it plays out in his brothers' betrayal. David's sin with Bathsheba introduces a level of deceit and violence into his family that culminates in Absalom's rebellion. Rehoboam breaks faith with the tribes when he is unwilling to listen to their legitimate complaints about the burdens the government of his father made them carry, and instead promises even heavier burdens. In nearly every case, such painful wounding or broken trust results in dire consequences, both for the leader involved and for the nation as a whole. The exact same is true in churches.

TRUST AND THE NATURE OF A BODY

We find evidence of a loss of trust for leadership in Paul's body analogy. "And the eye cannot say to the hand, 'I have no need of you'; or again the head to the feet, 'I have no need of you'" (1 Cor. 12:21). Notice that both the eye and the head are found at the top of the body while the hand and feet hold lower positions. Paul gives these body parts a voice to make a point. If the eye (those who may be entrusted with vision and direction) should say to any of the rest of the body, "I have no need of you," how would the hands or the rest of the body respond? If the head (those who may be entrusted with leading) should say to the feet, "I have no need of you," would not the feet and the rest of the body feel less inclined to put their faith in the head's commands? Any leader telling a follower, "I have no need of you" probably wounds the one they were called to serve. This injured part of the body reacts at first by hesitating to put its faith in the one so insensitive, and if it goes on the hands and feet stop trusting the eye and the head completely, until something is done to reconcile and heal the relationship.

Paul's letters to the Corinthians demonstrates the importance of trust for leaders in the Body of Christ. The Corinthian's faith in Paul appears to hang in the balance, but it may have more to do with their past experiences with authority than with any misbehavior of the apostle. Paul writes in 2 Corinthians 7:2, "Make room for us in your hearts; we wronged no one, we corrupted no one, we took advantage of no one." Was it that Paul fails to visit their church when he said he would that upset the Corinthian believers or does it just seem to confirm something that they believe their leaders will always do to them? It is also clear that Paul's first letter wounds the Corinthians churchgoers, but is it because Paul has done something wrong or do they bring a wounded spirit into their relationship with Paul and Christ that the first letter exposes?[10] They react to his chastisement with criticism, suggesting Paul is not all he is cracked up to be.[11] For these, and perhaps other reasons, Paul spends a lot of time explaining his ministry and seeking to reconcile with them.[12] Again we can compare the Corinthian's suspicion toward Paul with the attitude of the Jerusalem church toward the apostles: "They were continually devoting themselves to the apostles teaching."[13] Which church do you think had more trust in its leadership, and therefore had a stronger, healthier ministry?

Because of the systemic nature of the local church body, a lack of trust never shows up in just a single dimension of church life. A loss of trust in leadership wreaks havoc throughout the whole system. Patrick Lencioni writes, "Teams that lack trust waste inordinate amounts of time and energy managing their behaviors and interactions within the group. They tend to dread team meetings and are reluctant to take risks in asking for or offering assistance to others. As a result morale on distrusting teams is usually quite low

---

[10] 2 Cor. 10:9: 2 Cor. 7:8
[11] 1 Cor. 4:19-20; 2 Cor. 10:10-11
[12] 2 Cor. 3:1 and throughout 2 Corinthians
[13] Acts 2:42

and unwanted turnover is high."[14] If that is what happens in a secular workplace, think about the implications for the Body of Christ. A lack of trust undermines communication, even as we see that Paul has to explain what he's said and why he has said it to the Corinthians. A lack of trust hampers people from working together to achieve whatever mission or vision God gives a church to accomplish. Such a lack of trust, if unaddressed, will erode the spirit or corporate pulse of a church. And a lack of trust for human leaders often leads to a lack of trust toward God Himself Who called those leaders and put them in place. Many churches feel complete freedom to begin a pattern of firing those God may have called, without asking Him for His opinion. As a result His blessing on such churches fades like an afternoon shadow as unbelief grows over time.

We usually think that the most common break in trust occurs between a congregation and its pastor, but that's not always the case. It can work the opposite way too. If a congregation wounds its pastor or his family, the pastor begins to doubt he is safe with the flock he leads. He may start a series of self-protective behaviors, running the gamut from isolating himself in his study to avoid being hurt to searching for another position. A loss of trust can also impact a church's staff. If the staff feels a heavy handed management style by the elders or pastor, they hesitate to do more than what's required of them. If they feel they have no voice and no safe avenue to lodge a concern, they too may start sending out resumes. Additionally, if lay leaders feel mistreated or abused by the pastor, they might submit for a while, but they also may create an organized backlash to rid themselves of him, and protect themselves from any future pastor, because they have learned not to trust pastors. You can see that trust in leadership plays a vital role in the health and functioning of your church. Without it, there is

---

[14] Patrick Lencioni, *The Five Dysfunctions of a Team* (San Francisco: Josey-Bass, 2002) 196.

little or no forward progress as spiritual vitality gets undermined by suspicion.

UNREPAIRED BREACHES

To complicate things further, when broken trust goes unresolved, it remains in the system. People remember it. It tends to overshadow all subsequent leaders, even if they were not among the original offenders. Parishioners will project their deficit of trust even on newly appointed or called leaders, and the distrust will remain until something is done to heal the distrust.

When a lack of trust toward leadership exists in a congregation, anxiety/fear replaces peace as a defining characteristic of the church. When shepherds are perceived as untrustworthy, the sheep get skittish. They prove less willing to follow and more suspicious about the intent of leaders who try to lead, often resisting their leadership efforts and initiatives. The distrust gets reinforced with every new or imagined trust violation. The unhappiness this produces builds to the point of crisis, often an explosion set off by something small or insignificant.

One church with which Blessing Point consulted came to us with historical problems that included financial indiscretion on the part of one leader and an inability to work with their pastor, no matter who he was. Amazingly, the financial troubles and brief pastoral tenures plagued the church's history for *one hundred years!* The average stay of a senior pastor during their history was only *three* years. How hard would it be for a church to trust their pastor when he seems ready to leave on the next bus? On the other side of the coin, what does a long series of short pastoral tenures say about the difficulty of shepherding such a church?

The same lack of trust showed up in another church but for different reasons. We were called to work with a large church of

2000 after an ugly blow up between the deacons and a newly hired senior pastor. The staff responded to his hire by throwing their support behind the new senior pastor, who, even in his short tenure, had encouraged them more than the former pastor had, investing in them and building them up. This stood in sharp contrast to the treatment the staff received at the hands of the deacons who sought to manage them like hirelings. Problems among associate pastoral staff went back three decades in that church. The buildup of unresolved trust found explosive expression about every ten years, usually in an ugly crisis, an exodus, or a split.

In both these churches (and in most churches where we see it), lack of trust manifests itself in periodic internal crises. These cycles of pain occur apart from what might be considered healthy numerical growth. One might expect that such trust issues would create a state of decline, but attendance-wise, both churches I described held their own. That was part of what fooled people and led to leaders who were unwilling to change. They both looked impressive from the outside, but internally they faced painful challenges that impacted their church's functioning. And sooner or later the challenges they face will resurface in a blow-up from which recovery will be unlikely. Mars Hill Church in Seattle stands as a well-documented example of this kind of collapse.

Pastors, staff, lay leaders and congregation work well together only when trust permeates the relationships between the various parties. Lencioni writes, "Trust is the confidence among team members that their peer's intentions are good, and that there is no reason to be protective or careful around the group."[15] Insert a speck of doubt about leaders' intentions or actions and spontaneous cooperation begins to slow or stall as people become careful or self-protective. Those leading the body suddenly feel as if they've suffered a

---
[15] Ibid 19.

neurological short circuit. The body either no longer reacts to the head's instructions or responds haltingly at best.

REVIEW

Whether your church body trusts its leadership (or not) is a basic determiner of the health of your church. Trust is the currency of leadership, the "coin" of God's realm, and an absolute necessity for churches to function in a healthy way. How would leaders in your church answer these questions found on our ChurchScan Inventory:
- Are lay leaders and the congregation open to pastoral initiatives?
- Is the pastoral staff and congregation open to board initiatives?
- Is your church free from reactive, resistant behavior toward leadership?
- Are your church business meetings pleasant, positive and non-conflicted?
- Are your church leaders free from a need to control the congregation?

CHAPTER 7

Sphere Three - Mission/Vision Fulfillment

The story goes that a motorist, lost on a back road in Alabama, asked the way to Montgomery. An old farmer, sitting on a fence, looked down the road, scratched his head and gave explicit directions. Half an hour later, after following the farmer's directions carefully, the motorist found himself back at the starting point. The farmer was still sitting on the fence, in placid contemplation of the landscape. "Hey, what's the idea?" the motorist demanded indignantly. "I did just what you told me, and look where I wound up!" "Wal, young feller," the farmer explained, "I didn't aim to waste my time tellin' you how to git to Montgomery till I found out if you could follow simple directions."[16]

If you feel like you've cycled back into the mess where you started—in destructive conflicts, in congregational resistance toward leadership, in exoduses of people small and great—after carefully following the directions of the church growth/church health camp, then your church struggles at the level of mission/vision fulfillment and probably suffers deeper problems.

No church or church leader can escape the missional mandate the Lord of the Church left for his followers. Familiar Bible passages like Matthew 28:19-20 and Acts 1:8 spell it out. Jesus further made it clear that He expects churches to *complete* their God-given mission in the Seven Letters to the Churches in Revelation. He warned the

---

[16] *Bits & Pieces Magazine*, n.d.

church at Sardis: "I have not found your deeds completed in the sight of My God." The God who "created us in Christ Jesus for good works . . . that we should walk in them" (Eph. 2:10) clearly cares about the works of a church He created to walk in them as well. The church in Sardis, by failing to accomplish Christ's expectations, put their ministry in danger of extinction.

If your church struggles to gain missional traction, there are only a couple of possible explanations for your dilemma:

- Your church fails to keep its proper priorities and does not discern its unique assignment in the community where Christ placed you. He has a purpose for every church in every neighborhood in relation to the Gospel. You may need some coaching and equipping to grow your missional effectiveness, but once you discern God's path for your church the way becomes clearer. (This assumes that your church has become healthy enough to bear fruit.)
- Your church suffers underlying relational and spiritual problems that impede your church's ability to fulfil your mission. If this is the case, it matters not whether you have discerned Christ's unique purpose for your church. Systemic problems will produce a Sardis-type of situation where your church fails to do everything God set forth for you.

We want to examine how systemic malfunctions inhibit missional traction and explore how unseen spiritual hindrances prevent a church from producing fruit. We also want to compare the Jerusalem church (which was successful at its mission) and the church at Corinth (which was not). Corinth illustrates a significant cause of missional derailment. Finally, we will look at the impact of leaders who ignore the body's "signals" that something is wrong that hinders churches from fulfilling their unique calling. Once a church identifies and addresses the systemic issues affecting it, it's surprising how clear its mission becomes. However, until a church deals with its underlying problems, fulfilling its mission remains out of reach.

SPIRITUAL BLOCKS

Let's start by taking a look at unseen spiritual blocks to your church's fruitfulness. In Luke 13:6-9, we find the story of one frustrated farmer.

> A man had a fig tree which had been planted in his vineyard; and he came looking for fruit on it and did not find any. And he said to the vineyard-keeper, 'Behold, for three years I have come looking for fruit on this fig tree without finding any. Cut it down! Why does it even use up the ground?' And he answered and said to him, 'Let it alone, sir, for this year too, until I dig around it and put in fertilizer; and if it bears fruit next year, *fine*; but if not, cut it down.'

What was wrong with the unproductive fig tree? The aggravated owner of the vineyard saw problems with its lack of fruit; his astute vineyard-keeper, however, saw problems with the plant's roots. The gardener dug around the tree, applied fertilizer and gave the fig tree one more year of care. Many an unfruitful church is just like the unfruitful fig tree. It is clear that God has expectations and looks for its fruit. Churches, unlike believers, do not get eternal life, and He will shut them down or withdraw His Presence if they continue unfruitful.

Like the vineyard-keeper, perhaps we should do a little digging around the ministry to see if we can figure out what is causing such an issue. If a church suffers from prolonged ministry fruitlessness, people may think the problem is the pastor's leadership, the church's programs, or the board's policies. We believe you have to look deeper, to the roots of a church's spiritual functioning and its history. In 2 Samuel 21, David is 30 plus years into his own reign and discovered that something Saul did *literally* affected the fruit during his own reign 30 years later! A three-year famine prompted David to seek the Lord as to why God permitted this national pain. The Lord reveals that famine had nothing to do with anything David did, but that, Saul's actions, decades earlier, in killing off most of a people group with whom Israel had a covenant called the Gibeonites, so offended God that He blocked His blessing on the nation as a whole during David's reign. The famine was the instrument to communicate Divine unhappiness, something directly related to fruitfulness.

A "famine" on fruit in your church may likewise be a clue that something in your church's historical roots offends Him. Once David made amends for the sins of Saul, God's blessing on the nation returned. Sometimes churches need to take a deeper look at what might be preventing the fruitfulness before they can expect to make significant progress.[17]

We once had a plumbing problem in our house. There's no delicate way to put it. The downstairs toilet slowly stopped working. Talk about frustrating! When I removed the toilet from its mount, I discovered a perfect wreath around the drain pipe. The root of a pine tree made its way under the slab of our house, through a crack, and looped several times around the sewer line opening. The tree from which the root came stood at least thirty feet away!

Before I discovered the real cause for the blockage I did exactly what many churches and church leaders do with their fruitlessness. I wondered first if I needed all new equipment—a new commode. What unhappy work that would have required! Or maybe it was weak water flow that generated the problem and we needed to run

---

[17] For more on this topic read *Body Aches – Experiencing and Responding to God's Discipline of Your Church*, (Churchsmart 2009) by Kenneth Quick.

new and larger pipes. Perhaps there was a blockage, but running a roto-rooter snake down the line didn't solve the problem either; it only scratched the porcelain! All these "fixes" would prove misguided, and, in some cases, very expensive. Churches will replace staff, fire pastors, rewrite their constitutions, and change their structures—all for similar reasons. The reality though is that there is a totally unseen problem from a distant location, something that began years before, invaded the house and blocked the plumbing.

Churches with a long period of minimal fruitfulness should consider their situation from another angle. A church bears an intimate connection with Christ Himself. He sees reasons why a church struggles that we don't and a church needs to listen to Him! Perhaps it's time for a leadership paradigm shift instead of leadership replacement. As it relates to a church's ability to fulfill its mission or vision, if there's no fruit on the shoot, consider the *root!*[18]

SPIRITUALLY DRAINED

Another cause of missional derailment is evident in contrasting the health of the Jerusalem Church in Acts with problems in the church at Corinth. The Jerusalem church saturated their community with the Gospel. They evangelized, saw God do miraculous things, and baptized many – all while filled and empowered by the Holy Spirit. Multitudes came to Christ. They proved so effective that the unbelieving Jewish ruling class grew jealous and sought to squelch them. They accused the apostles of "filling Jerusalem with their teaching." From the apostles' perspective, they were fulfilling their God-given mission/commission. Even when persecution broke out and all the believers other than the apostles were scattered

---

[18] Further discussion of issues that impede missional traction can be found in *The Path of Revival – Restoring Our Nation One Church at a Time* (Churchsmart 2009) by Mark Barnard and *Healing the Heart of Your Church* by Kenneth Quick.

throughout the land, they *continued* to share the message and fulfill the commission.[19] Persecution didn't deter them, it *inspired* them.

As I described earlier, one reason they could focus on spreading the gospel grew out of their incredibly healthy corporate pulse. With the infusion of the Holy Spirit and the courage of the apostolic leadership, the Jerusalem church's vital signs were all strong. They were unified and devoted to the apostles' teaching, sacrificially loved each other, spent time in each other's homes, and shared Christ boldly. When threatened with sin in the camp, they implemented church discipline.[20] When the church started to come unglued through division, they found a solution that was Solomon-like in its wisdom as they added a layer of leadership that had previously not existed.[21] When persecution came, they stood tall.[22] They met every challenge in a God-honoring way without allowing it to turn into a church crisis. This is actually normative Christianity, where we see a church operating by means of all the things God has given to us as our birthright as His children.

The church at Corinth, sadly, looks much more modern. It displays a significant degree of spiritual immaturity. The questions the Corinthian church leaders put to Paul all focused on problems *within* the body. They asked questions like: "What is the right response to immorality in the church cause we have a little problem with it? How should we handle it when believers take each other to court? What should we do about our disunity around the Lord's Supper? Is it okay to buy and serve the cheap meat offered up in idol's temples? How can you say that our favorite spiritual gift might be dividing our church? Oh, and why is the resurrection so important anyway? By the way Paul, we're not really sure we trust you as a spiritual mentor anymore, would you mind justifying your

---

[19] Acts 8:1-4
[20] Acts 5:1-6
[21] Acts 6:1-7
[22] Acts 4: 5-12

role?"

The church at Corinth was so drained by their internal fractures, there is little mention of any outreach reflected in Paul's letters. The "sickness" the church body carried drained their energy for ministry outreach. How could a church, so preoccupied with internal squabbles, find the spiritual motivation to reach out? And who would want to bring a new believer into such a church?

When the human body gets infected by a virus, the immune system quickly goes into action. The rogue cells threatening the body get attacked by our built-in defense system. But while the battle rages over the infection, we often suffer a fever, sometimes a loss of appetite and energy. To expect our bodies to jump up and pursue their normal level of activity when we are sick proves unrealistic. Sometimes I have been on the tail-end of some bug that knocked me down but I convinced myself that I should get up and go back to work. I get out of bed, take a shower, and quickly discover that, because I'm not quite over whatever ails me yet, I have to fall back into bed.

Churches failing to fulfil their mission may be stalled because of that lack of spiritual maturity that keeps them operating like "mere men" and the energy drain from putting out fires. Thus a church like Corinth cannot impact their community as the church at Jerusalem did. They needed to first address the health of their church—something the apostle helps them do. He gives them Jesus' specific directions, directions we are *still* learning from as the Word of God. The Jerusalem church flourished because of the maturity of their leaders and the health of their fellowship. The leaders at Corinth needed a lot of mentoring. Paul knew it. He put up with their immaturity and tried to nurse them along. Thank the Lord, He doesn't quickly give up on any church.

SPIRITUALLY TONE DEAF

Finally, there are hints in Paul's body analogy that the church at Corinth failed to gain missional traction because its leaders failed to "discern the body rightly." They were taken up with dramatic or spectacular gifts of individual parts of the body, i.e. the head vs. the feet or the eye vs. the hand. They also valued the more "upfront" gifted parts of the body vs. those more private. We have not yet evolved beyond this. We think our church's problems reside in the fact that our pastor is not dynamic enough, or our youth pastor is not attracting enough young people, and the worship leader's voice is not good enough. This approach fails to discern what Jesus is saying to your church as a whole through the variously gifted parts of your body, especially the ones that are more quiet in their nature.

The Holy Spirit speaks through different parts of the body. His voice gets expressed through each part's unique giftedness and the sensitivities that giftedness provides. Someone with mercy gifts and justice gifts are absolutely crucial when dealing with a church discipline situation. A church and its leaders need to hear both attributes of God expressed through these spiritual gifts. He "sounds different" when He speaks through these different "parts" of the body, but it is the same God. What He says through someone with the gift of evangelism will sound different from what He says through someone else with the gift of teaching. Their focus and passion are very different, and the church needs *both* of them. What the Lord expresses through someone with the gift of administration (one who brings order to chaos) rings a different tone than when He speaks through someone with the gift of faith (who often wants to bypass order and operate spontaneously). God is in both, but the church often will value one over the other.

Their preoccupation with the spectacular resulted in the Corinthians failing to recognize how Christ speaks through and uses the different gifts to build up the body. They needed to take time to

SPHERE THREE - MISSION/VISION FULFILLMENT

assess all that the Spirit was saying to the church through all the gifted people God had provided to them so they could know His heart and be driven by His passion. If they had stepped back and done so, they would probably have had fewer questions for Paul, fewer divisions, and more mission fulfilment as every gifted person would be empowered to do what Christ had called them to do.

REVIEW

How well is your church fulfilling its mission/vision—the reason why Christ put you where you are? This is one area that stands as a great indicator of either God's blessing on your ministry or a red flag of warning about it. Do you know, pray about, and pursue with commitment the commission God has laid upon His Church and on your founders' hearts? How would leaders in your church answer questions like these:

- Are lay leaders excited and enthusiastic about the ministry of the church?
- Is your pastor and his family free from unhealthy stress related to his role in the church?
- Does your church experience a consistent sense of ministry effectiveness and momentum?
- Is your church accomplishing what Christ put it in your community to do?
- Does your church have many former leaders who are willing and eager to serve in the futures?

CHAPTER 8

<u>Sphere Four – Communication</u>

One evening a husband returned home from work and had the following conversation with his wife:

WIFE: "There's trouble with the car. It has water in the carburetor."
HUSBAND: "Water in the carburetor? That's ridiculous."
WIFE: "I tell you the car has water in the carburetor."
HUSBAND: "You don't even know what a carburetor is. Where's the car?"
WIFE: "In the swimming pool."[23]

The husband knows that his wife has little experience with carburetors. He therefore doubts her assessment of the car's problem. The wife knows that her husband has no idea what she knows about the car's location. However, for obvious reasons she avoids coming straight out with the upsetting news. How many conversations about what's wrong in church begin with assumptions of ignorance and dance around the real issues because they may be painful? Our experience is that there are way too many of them.

In churches with a high degree of dysfunction, making assumptions and dancing around elephants in the room goes on every day. Systemic difficulties play out in the relationships among members of the body, the staff and the boards included. Communication—healthy or unhealthy—shapes those relationships and defines life in

---
[23] *Reader's Digest ("Executive Speechwriter Newsletter," n.d.)*

the pews. When systemic health problems dominate, communication heats up and speeds up, but understanding slows to a crawl. Like those old dance contests where couples competed for prizes based on how long they could stay on their feet, leadership and parishioners will dance around painful issues as long as humanly possible.

When it comes to assessing communication in the local church, we want to pay attention to two things. First, how do unhealthy communication patterns take shape in the body? Second, how do we handle conflictual communication in a way that can ultimately honor God and be healthy for us?

UNHEATHY COMMUNICATION

Examples of unhealthy communication are abundant in the Scriptures. Revisiting Paul's body analogy in 1 Cor. 12, the various parts of the body talk to each other and not too nicely! The foot says, "Because I am not a hand, I am not a part of the body." The ear echoes the same sentiment, "Because I am not an eye, I am not a part of the body." These "appendages" betray a sense of inferiority when they compare themselves with other body parts. Others are saying "I have no need of you!" to their fellow body-parts. Instead of having an open conversation, valuing the differences between their varying roles, they nurse their grudges to the point of dismemberment.

Lencioni writes, "When team members do not openly debate and disagree about important ideas, they often turn to back channel personal attacks, which are far nastier and more harmful than any heated argument over issues." We see local churches suffer from this kind of behavior frequently. It's amazing how quickly communication deteriorates into reactivity in an unhealthy body. Like an autoimmune disease that attacks healthy tissue in its own body, mistaking healthy tissue for pathogens, the local body of

Christ can and does turn on itself. Paul told the Galatians "If you bite and devour one another, take care that you are not consumed by one another" (Gal. 5:15).

In Paul's letter to the Colossians he warns them about another threat to healthy communication: a power play by someone who wants influence. A teacher entered that community espousing certain rules and regulations to govern believers' lives and ultimately their acceptance by God. When Paul speaks of this false teacher, he describes him as "taking his stand on visions he has seen, inflated without cause by his fleshly mind, *not holding fast to the head*" (italics mine – Col. 2:18-19). The "head" in this case refers, not to church leadership, but to the Head of the church - Jesus Christ.

Interestingly, in Paul's analogy, the foot, ear, eye, and head base their value on their *function*, rather than basing it on Whose body they're a part of. Two body parts, the foot and the ear, wallow in self-pity, wishing they had someone else's gift. The other two parts, the eye and the head, glory in their superiority. Additionally, Paul depicts the false *teacher* in Colossae as being enamored with himself and his visions. It seems a church sometimes predisposes itself toward communication problems when a member's identity rests in their function, rather than in Christ Himself.

SOURCES OF UNHEALTHY COMMUNICATION

Where do unhealthy patterns of communication come from? I think we can safely say they all derive from our sin natures. But more than that, they often come from believers who lack a strong identity in Christ. Then we often act out (at church) many of the unhealthy communication styles we learned in our families of origin. Did you have issues with and anger toward authority growing up? You may find it natural to take on that role in the congregation, questioning the motives or decision-making of the lay leadership or pastoral staff. Did you avoid conflict at home? If that's how you were trained, don't be surprised if you default to the same approach in the church. Perhaps you grew up in a home where conflict escalated into angry outbursts. You'll face the same temptation at church! In fact, displaying any one of these approaches at church may feel entirely natural to you because of your upbringing.

Because we bring all of who we are into the Body of Christ, our old ways of handling communication and conflict come with us and Christ keeps working with us as we mature to break these "old ways." Are you aware of any carry-over of your old life into your ministry context? Do you find yourself reacting to certain members of the church like you reacted to a certain family member growing up? The Corinthians had a lot of this kind of growing up to do. All the spiritual gifts show up in their church; what they lack is the maturity to relate to each other in a healthy way. It is not without significance that the chapter immediately after Paul's detailed body analogy in 1 Corinthians 12 is the "Love Chapter" of 1 Corinthians 13. Paul goes to great lengths to enlighten the Corinthian believers about what mature love looks like in the context of relationships and communication.

BLESSABLE CONFLICT

Where can we find a model of handling communication and conflict in a way that God can bless? The answer rests in the larger context of Paul's two letters to the Corinthians. Keep in mind how systemically unhealthy this church was. Paul steps into the middle of the conflicted situation without becoming reactive, without ignoring their problems, and without giving up on them! But he also will not let them alone about the nature of what is going on in their midst.

A bird's eye view of these two letters illustrates Paul's willingness to engage in healthy communication. Such communication is sometimes painful, necessary but painful. He faced hard issues with

SPHERE FOUR - COMMUNICATION

direct words, but never with cruel intent. Paul models the kind of spirit we need to keep healthy communication flowing in the church, even when things are conflicted and tough.

Trace the way Paul communicates with them. His first letter moves from graciousness (1 Cor. 1:1-9) to exhortation (1 Cor. 1:10-17), to vulnerability (1 Cor. 2:1-5), to admonishment (1 Cor. 4:14-21), to confrontation (1 Cor. 5), to correction (1 Cor. 6-10), to praise (1 Cor. 11:2), to the withdrawal of praise (1 Cor. 11:17-22), to instruction (1 Cor. 12-16), and ends with an affirmation of love (1 Cor. 16:24). Unshackled by the need to please or the fear of man, Paul addresses these difficult issues without being abusive.

The same pattern of engagement occurs in Paul's second letter, though he does have to substantiate his credentials for the skittish Corinthian congregation. They obviously were not accustomed to such directness from their leaders. For much of 2 Corinthians, Paul's tone sounds softened by his experiences of suffering and hardship, but he still speaks the truth in love to them. Toward the end, Paul becomes more assertive (2 Cor. 10). He defends and justifies his ministry and apostolic authority with them (2 Cor. 11-12). In Chapter 13 He threatens to use a rod on them when he comes, issues a warning (13:10), and ends with gracious wishes for the church (vs 11-14).

Paul consistently deals with conflictual issues by communication born of *affection*. He clearly wants the best for this church, which is always the requirement of the servant-heart when in authority. Authority exists to make life better for those under authority. Paul uses his apostolic authority to set limits, define reality, and lead them away from trouble. But he also displays compassion with his candor. He works not to damage the fruit or bruise those church members and situations he must confront. At the same time he pulls no punches and challenges the contentious to retreat. It is a magnificent dance of all the graces at work at once.

You (and your church leadership) may be uncomfortable with honest communication. You may feel like you just don't know how to do it in your "minefield" situation. Some of us are all heart and hesitate to speak the truth. Some of us enjoy confrontation while not always manifesting a loving spirit. Paul models truth *and* love because they flow out of the life experiences that shape him. God trusts Paul with his role as an apostle because He knows Paul's heart, and He lets the apostle model the right way of doing things.

The unsaved bully, Saul of Tarsus, who liked to throw his weight around and didn't care who he hurt had the grace of God get firm control of his heart when he met the resurrected Christ. Jesus softened his heart through the years and reshaped him. As a result, he could still be firm about the truth as he dealt with his charges without being harsh or mean spirited, and love them in the manner of 1 Corinthians 13. Modern church leaders must aspire to this kind of healthy Christian communication in their ministries.

REVIEW

Healthy communication is crucial to a healthy church, like nerve signals which permit all body parts to operate as they should without paralysis or insensitivity or hypersensitivity. Moreover, in a healthy church, the head (however your leadership structure defines it) listens to the body and what all its parts have to say on issues that are relevant to them.

On the other side, without an atmosphere characterized by open, truthful, loving communication, conflicts seldom get resolved or reconciled. Bad feelings build and go underground, fueling the engines of gossip and destructive criticism. Unhealthy churches *always* have unhealthy and/or painful patterns of communication. It is one of the great symptoms of a weakened body.

The unhealthy expressions and behaviors will move back and forth

SPHERE FOUR - COMMUNICATION

from overt to covert, distorting how your church functions. At its worst, "elephants" will fill whatever room you are in and no one will talk about the things that desperately need to be addressed. Consider the quality of communication in your church, by reflecting on the following questions:

- Do your pastor, staff and lay leaders feel safe discussing difficult issues with each other?
- When your leaders know real problems exist, do they talk about them? Are there any elephants in the room?
- Do your leaders resolve their interpersonal conflicts in a godly and timely manner?
- Do your church's leaders courageously and consistently address church discipline issues?
- Are you currently free from unhealthy/destructive interpersonal tension within the church?

CHAPTER 9

Sphere Five – Historical Wounds

In the late 1970's, a new church in a growing suburban area fired their pastor of two years over alleged immorality. Part of the congregation reacted to the pastor's dismissal by establishing a new church eight miles down the road. The daughter church progressed along for about five years, until simmering distrust erupted in conflict with the first pastor they had called. He and his family left wounded and discouraged. The church muddled on through a series of short-lived pastorates until one shepherd, whose strong personality and acumen for political maneuvering, kept him at the helm for fifteen years. The church grew exponentially! However, the dynamic pastor's tenure came to an abrupt halt when news of an ongoing immorality came to light. As a result, half the congregation left to start a new church in another part of town.

This church's sad, cyclical tale reminds me of the lyrics to Harry Chapin's song, "The Cat's in the Cradle." Chapin's haunting lines tell the tale of a father who just can't "find the time" to get involved in his son's life. As his son grows up, the tables turn and the father longs for a place in his son's busy life. The neglect of the father toward the son becomes the neglect of the son toward the father. The pattern will likely continue, repeating itself through the generations, until someone rights the relational dysfunction. Chapin concludes the song with, "As I hung up the phone it occurred to me he'd grown up just like me; my boy was just like me." The difference is we are dealing with moral issues here, and testimony issues of what Christians are really like before a watching world. Is it any wonder that the church is seen as less and less relevant today? How do we overcome such repeated patterns of corporate ugliness?

We call these events "historical wounds." They effect profoundly the systemic health of local churches. In this chapter, we want to explore the kinds of crises and events that inflict such wounds on an entire congregation. Additionally, we must note how these corporate wounds take on special significance when they start to repeat themselves. Finally, we need to examine how unhealed corporate wounds impact the other four spheres of church life.

When we talk about "corporate wounds in the body of Christ," what are we talking about? Typically these are crises that impact the congregation as a whole. Here is a far from exhaustive list:
- A church split
- Abuse of a church by its pastor
- Abuse of a pastor by the church
- Sinful reactivity i.e, lashing out (in board meetings, worship services, business meetings, etc.
- Shameful events (e.g. racial prejudice, socioeconomic snobbery, silence in the face of wrongdoing.)
- Moral failure by a leader

In the opening story, the church in question suffered several of these corporate wounds mentioned in our list. In our work, we have seen many such churches with stories just as painful, if not worse. Here are a just a few variations: One church gets a reputation for "unspiritual lay leadership," having undermined a succession of pastors over the course of forty years. In another church, decades of lay leaders overlook a senior pastor's sense of entitlement and abuse. Yet another splits, and splits, and splits yet again. Still another has a succession of immoral pastors for 35 years. We've seen all these scenarios and more. Some occur in churches

SPHERE FIVE – HISTORICAL WOUNDS

on the backroads of rural America, others make front page news in the cities or suburbs where they dwell. Wherever they occur, they create a corporate wound and they injure the whole fabric of the Christian community associated with them.

Unhealed corporate wounds compromise healthy systemic functioning. If the ear, in Paul's body analogy, receives a direct, damaging blow, the whole body gets thrown off balance. If, as a result of the injury, the body falls to the ground, the eye is now limited in its capacity to do its job. How can the eye help a body see when face down against the pavement? Why would the foot threaten to leave the body as it does in 1 Corinthians 12:15 and what would be the impact if it did? Unhealed wounds in one part of the body effect the functioning of the whole, because if that foot leaves, the body will not be able to function very well.

The church at Corinth suffered real pain as a partisan spirit invaded the church. Battle lines were drawn around spiritual gifts, between haves and have-nots, and between favorite teachers. Some got labeled second-class citizens because they lacked certain spiritual gifts and or were labeled "weak" because they did not have the freedom others possessed. The pain such wounding produces is collective—people together share it in different ways, but almost all feel it. Some are disgusted, some are angry, some are just hurt, some walk away and some run. Apart from reconciliation that pain and hurt stays within the body, showing up (usually cyclically) to remind everyone that unhealed history repeats itself. Thus systemic dysfunction and pain becomes chronic, and the body continues to carry it.

How these problems get handled by the church leaders can differ greatly. Sadly, most churches gloss over their painful corporate history, but true health demands they consider their previous spiritual journey. They need to hear what Jesus is saying to their church just like those churches in Revelation 2-3, and then do what

He tells them. They need to hear and understand the context of Haggai's call for the Israelites to *consider their ways*, because like Israel, they are experiencing similar types of corporate pain (Hag. 1:2-11). When major sources of pain enter the life of the church, rather than putting it behind us or under some church rug, perhaps we should ask Gideon's question, "If the Lord is with us, why then has all this happened to us?" (Judges 6:13) Some church leaders assume that, if you are operating all the right programs, then blessings and progress will surely follow. That wasn't the way the people of Haggai's day found it. Corporate repentance and corporate healing may be required before true church health, and possible pastoral longevity and fruitful progress can occur.

REPETITIVE WOUNDINGS

Our experience, seen in just about every church with which we have worked, is that corporate wounds often fail to receive adequate treatment and healing because modern church leaders do not understand the systemic nature of them or the role of leadership in healing them. A new pastor may come on the scene, get everyone excited, calm down the painful things momentarily, and try to begin anew. But this is not healing, and that is the deception contained in it. Because there is a brief moment of excitement and pain-free experience corporately, as soon as the pain starts up again (and it *always* does) the church concludes it is the "new pastor's fault" and unceremoniously remove him to get yet another new pastor to provide the brief interlude from pain again. The cyclic time period for this may be as short as six months or as long as four to five years, but it always happens.

Such churches get known as "pastor killers" in their denominations. This is an extreme condition, but we have watched the same kinds of problems repeat themselves in the church's experience. This happened in Israel as well, as we see Jeremiah saying, "They have healed the brokenness of My people superficially, saying, 'Peace,

SPHERE FIVE – HISTORICAL WOUNDS

peace,' but there is no peace" (Jer. 6:14). You don't need a seminary degree to know how Israel's problems repeated themselves throughout their history and how God's discipline of them increased their corporate pain to try to get them to turn around.

Edwin Friedman, in his classic book on church and family systems called *Generation to Generation*, cites a medical illustration to explain how superficial healing causes more problems, not less. He writes:

> When a physical wound occurs there are two kinds of tissue that must heal, the connective tissue below the surface, and the protective tissue of the skin. If the protective tissue heals too quickly, healing of the connective tissue will not be sound, causing other problems to surface later, or worse, never to surface at all.[24]

The same proves true for wounded churches. While things might look fine momentarily on the surface, unhealed hurts linger below, and the devil takes advantage of their unseen presence as a beachhead and will stir things up at a strategic time (for him). The same old wounds resurface in the form of fresh crises, and are separated by years or even decades, but they are the exact same, whether caused by broken trust (the most common) or the pastor treated as a hireling or a controlling individual. With the repetition and escalation of this congregational pain, the church quickly gets robbed of any spiritual vitality.

Because of the church's spiritual nature, the repetition of corporate wounds tells another story also. If unhealed wounds linger in a church of believers, we must consider the reality that the Lord not

---

[24] Friedman Edwin H, *Generation to Generation*. New York: Guilford Press; 1985:43-45.

only knows these wounds exist, He has *permitted them*. Don't misunderstand what I say here. I believe He watches and grieves as they repeat themselves, but the crucial thing to understand is that the Lord of your church *allows* them.

Having said that, it is also crucial to understand that, He is *never silent* about such things, speaking through the crises themselves, even as He used to speak to Israel through their droughts and locust plagues. He allows painful events to repeat themselves *to alert church leaders to injuries below the surface* that remain unrectified and unhealed. Make no mistake, He longs for His "body" to be healed and for leaders to learn the spiritual lessons contained in the pain they repetitively encounter, but He will never overlook His righteous standards in the context of the local churches which represent Him and His name in a community.

Quick, in his book *Healing the Heart of the Church*, says, "God keeps taking His people around and around through similar experiences until they finally learn the lessons that allow them to make further progress. Could this explain your church's problems in the present? Are they taking yet another trip around Mt. Sinai?"[25] It's a question every church must consider as they assess their systemic health in relation to historical crises, especially when you find in your ministry's history repeated examples of similar events.

INTERRELATED IMPACT

How does the sphere of historical wounds impact the other four spheres of systemic functioning? Of the five spheres of systemic health in the local church, historic corporate wounds contain the most potential for damaging the ongoing wellbeing of your church. While all five spheres impact each other, and problems in any of the

---

[25] *Healing the Heart of Your Church* p 23.

SPHERE FIVE – HISTORICAL WOUNDS

spheres need attention, historical wounds provide the most significant indicator of the state of your church's true spiritual health. Their absence suggests you may simply have an isolated problem in another sphere that can be addressed with a practical solution. The presence of unhealed corporate wounds in the history, however, always predicts that there will be ongoing (and deepening) problems in your church. Here are some of the ways unhealed wounds effect the other spheres of systemic health.

Corporate Pulse: While listening to sports radio in the car one day, I heard a story about a college football team from Washburn University in Topeka, Kansas. Unlike many familiar mascots like the Bulldogs, Eagles, or Warriors; Washburn University decided to name their team after their school's generous benefactor, Ichabod Washburn. Yes, the school's football team is known as the *Ichabods*. It is hard to believe that a university would name its team after an Old Testament word that means "the glory has departed." They may as well have named them the Washburn Losers! What an odd choice.

For many churches though, the lingering presence of unhealed wounds leaves them feeling like the glory of God has departed from them as well. (Do we dare call them Ichabod churches?) They almost always look back on "glory days" as things in the past. They now march into spiritual battle like Samson with his head shaved, not realizing God's Presence has departed and that He now stands outside their fellowship knocking, waiting for someone to hear His voice (Rev. 3:20). It may not happen all at once, but in churches where such unhealed wounds go untreated, the church's corporate pulse *wanes*. The kind of joyful spirit evidenced in the Jerusalem church in Acts 2 seems a distant dream. Over time they become part of a little known, but extremely large denomination, the AOI – The Assemblies of Ichabod.

Trust in Leadership: Distrust of authority hangs in the air of our culture. The roots of our distrust in public figures, politicians in particular, can easily be traced to their letting us down in the past. We come to trust *no* politicians. The cumulative effect across the population of our "once bitten, twice shy" reaction leaves our nation floundering.

The same thing occurs in a church where a leader—pastoral or lay—wounds the congregation in some fashion. We also see it when people transfer into your church from a setting where they were wounded by other church leaders. Wounded believers don't trust *any* leader (even reliable, faithful, and trustworthy ones) once they've been "bitten." They tend to see them all as dangerous, view them with suspicion, and respond to them out of their pain. Such is the sad situation we see on a regular basis in our consulting ministry. We have to teach leaders how to heal such breaches of trust between a former leader and those who follow, because they often have no clue.[26] We have written extensively on the subject elsewhere.[27] Suffice it to say, unhealed corporate wounding leads to broken trust in church leaders.

Mission/Vision Fulfillment: There are two primary ways unhealed historical wounds hinder mission and vision fulfillment. First, wounded churches get preoccupied with the various symptoms of their injuries. Church leaders spend their time putting out relational fires, wrestling with declining offerings, or trying to fix repetitive church crises. We see this at the denominational level as well as District Superintendents or Directors of Mission have much of their time consumed by dealing with such churches instead of what they really want/feel called to do, which is help churches achieve the Great Commission. But in wounded churches, leaders lack the energy to pursue new initiatives to move their vision for the church

---

[26] Visit blessingpoint.org to learn how we can help to mend the fabric of your church.
[27] See "Other Resources to Help Your Church" p 101.

SPHERE FIVE – HISTORICAL WOUNDS

forward. The majority of their energy gets consumed by their sickness and injury. Such systems are rarely efficient or high octane. They are more often "black holes" for spiritual energy and drag others down with them. How then can the local church leaders or denominational leaders find the additional energy to advance the mission of their church?

Second, the wounds most churches receive are caused by someone *sinning against the corporate body*. We all deal with sin every day, but it is different when a leader or group of leaders do something (or fail to do something) that causes a wound in the corporate body. Ultimately leaders are responsible before God for *whatever* happens under their watch (Heb. 13:17). If they misuse their authority in any way or violate moral boundaries in the context of their leadership role, or if they fail to protect the congregation from the many things that can do them damage spiritually, it breaks trust and creates a corporate wound. The categories of such events and sins are listed on (page 72).

When sin enters the Body of Christ and goes untreated, we are left with a situation similar to Achan and the sin he brought into the Israelite camp—there is a *corporate* impact. Unless you believe that, as New Testament believers, God now overlooks "sin in the camp," then it becomes unrealistic to expect God to bless the mission of a church when church leaders overlook sin's presence. This is why Paul fusses with the Corinthians in 1 Corinthians 5. The leaders have not dealt with something extremely dangerous to the body. In such cases, not only do churches need to heal the wounds caused by the leaders or individuals involved, **but they must right the church's relationship (as a whole) with God – before they can expect to make missional progress**. Healing is not an option, it is a necessity and leaders must learn how to do it. They will not make progress until they do.

Communication: Why do people who have known each other at church for years suddenly stop talking to each other? Something painful has occurred between them to alienate one party from the other. In other cases folk may not stop talking completely, but learn to avoid certain painful topics. Wounded churches rarely risk talking about the issues that led to their being wounded. They fear the emotion that might resurface and feel that the wound cannot be healed. They don't want to be hurt further with no positive purpose. It's just not worth the risk. We especially witness this unwritten code of silence in churches influenced by cultural heritages where people have been trained to avoid conflict or to keep it "inside." I call this the "Hoover Vacuum" approach to communication – just suck it up! The end result is the issues never get faced and communication is always limited and unsafe.

The presence of unhealed corporate wounds gets evidenced by this fear of communicating about the painful issues and often drives unhealthy communication such as gossip. When healthy communication wanes, the impact soon gets felt church-wide. The church's pulse, trust in leaders, and missional fulfilment all suffer. Wounds continue to occur. Just as the five spheres of systemic health feed off each other for good, so also, like a bad shot in golf "begetting" another bad shot, a church's health deteriorates as untreated dysfunction in one sphere spreads to the other spheres.

REVIEW

Historical crises and a pattern or cycle of unresolved corporate trauma, represents the single most significant indicator of the need for healing in a church. These wounds rarely get addressed in churches because leaders are not trained to do it and don't know how it could be done. Moreover, leaders seldom realize how this damage is carried going forward. Very few churches will connect their present crisis with any past crisis or painful events. The reality is though that an unresolved crisis acts like a rip in the fabric of your church that, unrepaired, will further unravel with each new

SPHERE FIVE – HISTORICAL WOUNDS

problem.

God has made spiritual leaders responsible for this. To evaluate if your church suffers from unhealed historical trauma, how would you and the rest of your leaders answer the following questions:

- Is our church's history free of stories of bad behavior by previous pastors, boards or staff?
- Is our church's history free of injuries/wounds committed against previous pastors, boards or staff?
- Was our church birthed without controversy or from a split?
- Is our church currently free of trauma or corporate pain?
- Is our church free from any repetitive history (cycle) of corporate pain.

CHAPTER 10

The ChurchScan Inventory™

Based on what we've covered so far, be honest: How healthy is your church? We hope that the questions at the end of each of the previous chapters related to the five spheres of systemic functioning have gotten you thinking. It is wise for every leader in your church to answer those questions prayerfully, then engage in a frank discussion about your church's true health. It is a great focus for a board or staff retreat, or the first half hour discussion in board meetings for several months.

The questions are derived from what we at Blessing Point call our "ChurchScan Inventory." You can facilitate the process of assessing your church's health by having your leaders take the scan at **churchscaninventory.com**. You can also find a link to it on our website at **blessingpoint.org**. The online survey will document and collate your answers and provide you with overall recommendations for what can help you. We provide you with a link to your results, so you can review them at any time. This is a free service, our ministry to you.

Additionally if you'd like to have all your leaders fill out the survey and receive composite scores, we can facilitate that inexpensively. Simply contact us at info@blessingpoint.org to set it up. Otherwise, use the following paper version of the ChurchScan Inventory.

ChurchScan Inventory™

How accurate are the following statements as it relates to your church? Select only one answer for each question.

Scale: 1 – Not at all   2 – Some extent   3 – Great extent   4 – Very great extent

CORPORATE PULSE	1	2	3	4
Our congregation often has fun together, and joy is in the "atmosphere" when gathered.				
Our church leaders (pastoral, lay and staff) enjoy unity and love among themselves.				
God calls a good number of young people from our church into full-time ministry.				
Our church regularly sees conversions from its services and individual evangelism.				
Pastors at our church feel respected and enjoy long, positive tenures.				
Total Corporate Pulse:				

TRUST IN LEADERSHIP	1	2	3	4
Lay leaders and the congregation are open to pastoral initiatives.				
The pastoral staff and congregation are open to board initiatives.				
Our church is free from reactive, resistant behavior toward leadership.				
Our church business meetings are pleasant, positive, and non-conflicted.				
Our church's leaders are free from a need to control the congregation.				
Total Trust In Leadership:				

MISSION/VISION FULFILLMENT	1	2	3	4
Our lay leaders are excited and enthusiastic about the ministry of the church.				

THE CHURCHSCAN INVENTORY

Our pastor and his family are free from unhealthy stress related to his role in the church.				
Our church enjoys a consistent sense of ministry effectiveness and momentum.				
Our church is accomplishing what Christ put it in our community to do.				
Our church has many former leaders who are willing and eager to serve in the future.				
Total Mission/Vision Fulfillment:				
COMMUNICATION	1	2	3	4
Our pastor, staff and lay leaders feel safe discussing difficult issues with each other.				
When leaders know real problems exist they talk about them. No "elephants are in the room."				
Our leaders resolve their interpersonal conflicts in a godly and timely manner.				
Our church's leaders courageously and consistently address church discipline issues.				
We are currently free from unhealthy/destructive interpersonal tension within the church.				
Total Communication:				
HISTORICAL CRISES	1	2	3	4
Our church's history is free of stories of bad behavior by previous pastors, boards or staff.				
Our church history is free of injuries/wounds committed against previous pastors, boards or staff.				
Our church was birthed without controversy or from a split.				
Our church is currently free of trauma or corporate pain.				
Our church is free from any repetitive history (cycle) of corporate pain.				
Total Historical Crises:				
TOTAL OVERALL SCORE:				

Interpreting Your ChurchScan Results Per Category and Overall

CORPORATE PULSE:

Your Church's corporate pulse refers to those qualities normally found in healthy churches where Christ is present, honored, listened to, and followed. Passages like Acts 2:42-47 and 4:32-35 reveal the wonderful atmosphere or spirit God intended for your church (as a whole) to experience.

Low Corporate Pulse (Score 5-10) Churches that score low in Corporate Pulse face real danger. They likely reside on the downhill side of their life expectancy or are experiencing great pain/trauma. A low score should be cross-referenced with a church's score for Historical Crises. Painful events often give insight into why the church continues to struggle to enjoy unity and fruitfulness.

Action Point: Courageous leaders must embark on a journey to new life for their church. We have written two books, 1) *Healing the Heart of Your Church* by Ken Quick and 2) *The Path of Revival* by Mark Barnard to provide additional insight into how you can facilitate your church's return to spiritual health. If insufficient energy and commitment exists to revitalize your church, you may benefit from a resource like *Legacy Churches* by Stephen Gray & Franklin Dumond.

Medium Corporate Pulse (Score 11-15) Churches scoring in the medium range of Corporate Pulse have often reached a plateau or are starting to decline. Your church leaders need to give honest answers to questions like, "Have we lost our outward focus? Have we settled for the status quo? Is God happy with this and what does He want us to do about it?" Stability can be strength if it gets used to initiate new advances for the kingdom. However stability can also lead to stagnation if the goal becomes comfort.

THE CHURCHSCAN INVENTORY

Action Point: Danger signs exist and leaders must honestly discern if the pulse is getting stronger or weaker, if the congregation has a church growth/church health or systemic problem. Do there seem to be barriers you cannot get beyond? If so, underlying, systemic, issues may need to be addressed before healthy congregational life reemerges. *Healing the Heart of Your Church* by Ken Quick can help you solve these kinds of problems. If the church is free from a history of corporate pain, it may simply suffer a programmatic problem. A book like *Natural Church Development* by Christian Schwarz helps you get a handle on the factors conducive to improving your corporate pulse.

High Corporate Pulse (Score 16-20) Churches scoring in the high range of corporate pulse tend to be unified, healthy congregations. Joy is in the atmosphere and for the most part everyone rallies around what God is doing in your church.

Action Point: Keep up the good work by purposefully investing in the emotional and spiritual health of your leadership team. Consider a book like *The Emotionally Healthy Church* by Peter Scazzaro to strengthen your leaders along these lines.

TRUST IN LEADERSHIP:

Whether your church body trusts its leadership (or not) speaks volumes about the health of your church. Trust is the currency of leadership, the "coin" of God's realm, and an absolute necessity for churches to function in a healthy way. Sometimes though, a congregation will not trust current leaders, or boards won't trust pastors because of wounds received from other leaders in the past. The crux of this is that, if people do not trust their leaders, they will not follow them, so every leadership initiative gets resisted or openly opposed.

DIAGNOSING THE HEART OF YOUR CHURCH

Low Trust in Leadership (Score 5-10) A general lack of trust for your leaders exists in your church. It evidences itself on multiple levels. Leaders experience undue suspicion, control or power-seeking, or imagined or magnified offenses over issues that appear strange. These symptoms show up no matter who holds leadership positions in your church. We believe the roots of distrust for leaders will trace back to damage caused by a leader or leaders who broke trust in some way. It could have been a moral issue or a power-play. Churches with low trust experience episodes of corporate anxiety or hostility, an attitude of "they are up to something," and decreasing amounts of joy. Leaders who are not trusted often experience deteriorating physical, emotional, and spiritual health. The toll on their families is also high, sometimes alienating them from God and/or from participating in church life.

Action Point: Your church must review its history to identify the leadership failure(s) that broke the trust during the journey of your church. Once identified, these wounds must be treated using methods designed to heal the church as a whole. If hostility is too high, a consultant or intentional interim pastor (if the church is in transition) may be needed, someone who is experienced in helping a church regain trust for its leaders. Contact Blessing Point Ministries for help (blessingpoint.org).

Medium Trust in Leadership (Score 11-15)
Signs of mistrust exist for leaders in your church, but the culture of your church may not yet have been redefined by it. Leaders enjoy some degree of trust except, perhaps, in certain areas. There may be "hot-button topics," minefields that leaders have learned to avoid, which are explained when one understands the history of the church. Unaddressed, these trust issues tend to increase until there is a major rift or blow-up.

Action Point: The issue here is severity of the event(s) where trust may have been violated in your history. Review the history of your church to identify any such breaches of trust by current or former leaders. Even things suspected but unproven need to be addressed for trust to be restored. If leaders act to heal these wounds, trust will get "credited" to their account. Leaders will also have to make deposits into that account themselves with their behavior and in their communication with the congregation. If there are concerns about your ability to facilitate healing related to trust for leaders in your church, a consultant could help, so don't be afraid to contact Blessing Point Ministries for help (blessingpoint.org).

High Trust in Leadership (Score 16-20) The Scripture says, "Behold, how good and how pleasant it is for brothers (and sisters) to dwell together in unity!" Where trust for leaders is high, leaders enjoy positive, happy, lengthy tenures. Such leadership also produces growing, healthy congregations. Mutual trust and accountability between pastoral staff and lay leaders radiates out from there to the congregation. Leaders are followed and their initiatives received without resistance.

Action Point: The temptation faced by leaders with trust is to take inappropriate advantage of it, or to seek to be served rather than serve. Learn to protect and build up your bank account of trust by understanding how leaders lose it and how hard it is to rebuild once lost. Reading *Body Aches*, by Ken Quick can help. Review it with your leaders or bring in a Blessing Point Consultant to lead a one day seminar with your team.

MISSION/VISION FULFILLMENT:

How well are you fulfilling your church's mission/vision—the reason why Christ put you where you are? This is a great indicator of either God's blessing on your ministry or a red flag revealing His unhappiness with you. Do you as leaders know, pray about and pursue with commitment the mission/vision God has laid upon your hearts or on your founders' hearts? Failure to do so can be a clear symptom of the fabric of your church starting to unravel. Churches that are sick tend to use their energy and resources to get better—i.e. focus on themselves and not on reaching out. Underlying issues can subvert your best, most creative efforts at fulfilling all that God has in mind for your congregation.

Low Mission/Vision Fulfillment (Score 5-10) Jesus cares about mission/vision fulfillment. He told the church at Sardis, "I have not found your deeds complete in the sight of my God" (Rev. 3:2). If you score low in this area, the reasons can be three-fold: 1) You don't have a clearly defined mission/vision; 2) Your leaders are too worn out dealing with pain and problems to expend the necessary energy to pursue the mission/vision right now; or 3) The congregation resists leadership initiatives so you can seem to get untracked. You may be suffering from any or all of these issues, and thus your "deeds are incomplete." A lack of mission/vision fulfillment can cause high degrees of stress and discouragement if you as leaders keep trying to do the right things, yet cannot seem to get past the energy drain or congregational resistance.

Action Point: Many churches think that, if they have failed with one mission/vision, the answer is to create or redefine another one! Before embarking on a venture into identifying and implementing a new vision for your church, you must address the issues that have hindered leaders from achieving the mission/ vision you have. Ask God to reveal to you the real nature and reasons for the challenges you face (2 Sam. 21:1-3). The good news is that, if you really want to know, God can and will tell you. You must as leaders act to address these things first before God will help you achieve your mission/vision.

Medium Mission/Vision Fulfillment (Score 11-15) Jesus cares about mission/vision fulfillment and completing your works. He told the church at Sardis, "I have not found your deeds complete in the sight of my God" (Rev. 3:2). Your assessment results indicate that mission fulfillment is not as strong as it could be in your church. Though you have some strength in this area, you must discern what is slowing you down or holding you back, face these things honestly, and then you can move the church forward.

Action Point: Your church's leadership needs to ask itself some hard questions like: 1) Do we know why God put us in our community and can we articulate that clearly? 2) Does the congregation resist, overtly or covertly, following the mission/vision laid out by the leadership? This may be due to trust issues that you must address. 3) Do leaders have the energy and commitment they need to fulfill the mission/vision? The reasons for a lack in these areas must be clearly understood. These questions help you identify the source of the problem. New vitality is available to churches that take the time to hear from the Head of their church about what He wants them to do and what, if anything, needs to be corrected before God will bless your efforts to fulfill the purpose for your church.

High Mission/Vision Fulfillment (Score 16-20) Praise God! Your church continues to do a great job defining and fulfilling its mission and vision. Keep it up! A word of warning though: True vision fulfillment starts with a clear sense of what God wants us to do and then gets implemented by identifying the heaven-sent opportunities to fulfill the vision (Eph. 2:10). Beware of Nebuchadnezzar's pride (Dan. 4:30), taking credit for your success and thereby incurring the displeasure of the true Head of your church (Col. 2:19).

Action Point: Keep taking risks and stretching your faith. Beware of growing comfortable. Take time to learn how to better hear from God as a leadership team. Keep feeding the motivation to reach those around you.

COMMUNICATION:

Healthy communication is crucial to a healthy church, like the lifeblood circulating in a body or nerve signals which permit all parts to operate as they should without paralysis or insensitivity. Moreover, in a healthy church, the head (leadership) listens to the body. On the other side, without an atmosphere characterized by open, truthful communication, conflicts seldom get resolved or reconciled and bad feelings build and go underground, fueling the engines of gossip and criticism. Unhealthy churches always have unhealthy and/or painful patterns of communication. These expressions and behaviors move back and forth from overt to covert, distorting how your church functions. In its worst expressions, "elephants" fill whatever room you are in and no one will talk about the things that desperately need to be addressed.

Low Communication (Score 5-10) People do not feel free to discuss difficult topics in your church because they don't feel safe doing so. Unresolved conflicts prevent grace-filled communication! A cycle of increasing isolation and alienation ensues, seriously damaging and limiting any loving culture your church may possess. Because unresolved issues linger and build, reactive behavior will exhibit itself in informal and even formal church meetings. People may tolerate this only because they have never known the church to be any different.

Action Point: Handle with care, as churches with low scores are often a minefield for leaders! Before you can restore open communication and resolve conflicts in a healthy way, you must return to the source of the bad communication, the event(s) which started this way of behaving. Then you must take responsibility and confess this bad behavior to Christ and one another. Serious reflection is needed to evaluate exactly how the church arrived at this place. If leadership feels that they might not be able to control the unhealthy or critical communication to find out these things, an

THE CHURCHSCAN INVENTORY

outside, objective, facilitator can help lead your church through the healing process it needs. Feel free to contact us at Blessing Point Ministries (blessingpoint.org).

Medium Communication (Score 11-15) People do not always feel free or safe to discuss difficult topics in your church. Leaders must discern if this means people need training in conflict resolution (A book like *The Peacemaker* by Ken Sande could help.) or, if people's unwillingness to communicate comes from old congregational wounds that have not yet been healed. In the latter case, simply teaching on conflict resolution will fail to fix your church's communication problem, nor will restructuring or adding bylaws. Because communication is not as healthy as it could be, it becomes harder as leaders to do difficult things you may need to do, like church discipline. You may face episodes of unhelpful criticism and gossip. You may also witness occasions of reactive behavior in your church, where pent-up feelings come out more strongly than a situation warrants.

Action Point: Proceed with caution, but find the courage to proceed! You may need to explore the episodes of poor communication in your church to see if there is a pattern to them and when they started. They may be rooted in old conflicts or times when the congregation felt they had no voice. Consider working through a book like *Body Aches*, by Ken Quick on a leaders retreat to assess these things.

High Communication (Score 16-20) Your church operates with that rare quality of being safe and secure enough to "speak the truth in love." Leaders feel safe enough to discuss difficult issues with one another and congregational trust allows them to discuss such issues publicly. Your church could exercise church discipline if need be to keep the body healthy and free of infection. To have such a church is a great blessing. Guard carefully the atmosphere of trust you have and do not take it for granted.

Action Point: If your church is growing, be sure to restructure when communication lines get stretched to insure good avenues of communication stay open. Continue to build on your churches openness to communicate and confront problems by using a resource like *Peacemakers* by Ken Sande.

HISTORICAL CRISES:

Historical crises, and especially a pattern or cycle of unresolved trauma, represents the single most significant indicator of a need for healing in your church. These wounds seldom get addressed in churches because leaders are not trained to do it and seldom realize how churches carry such damage going forward. Your church may be in crisis now, but you may also know of crises it's faced in the past. An unresolved crisis acts like a tear in the fabric of your church that, un-mended, can further unravel with each new problem. If your church also scores low in the "Trust in Leadership" category, crises can result in splits, firings, petitions, or other highly unhealthy corporate behaviors.

Much Evidence of Historical Crises (Score 5-10) Your church has a painful past. The congregation may have experienced split(s), abuse of or by a church leader, sinful reactivity i.e. lashing out, shameful events i.e. racial prejudice or moral failure by a leader. All these, unrectified, have a long-term impact on your church body and its willingness to follow leadership. Your answers indicate that the wounds from these types of events in your church's history have yet to be healed. They prevent you from gaining any kind of traction in fulfilling your mission.

Action Point: Explore the consulting services Blessing Point Ministries offers to help you in this regard. We exist to help such churches. Seek the Lord for courage to face and repair the damage your church may have experienced. Ask Him to give you the courage to walk through a process of corporate healing. Such a process hold great hope for restoring your church to proper functioning.

Some Evidence of Historical Crises (Score 11-15) Your church shows some signs of having been wounded by a previous event(s). Your church may have experienced one of the following: a painful split, abuse of or by a church leader, sinful reactivity i.e. lashing out, shameful events i.e. racial prejudice, or it may have suffered a moral failure by a leader. If such a wound has yet to be healed, its effects will not go away unless leaders intentionally seek to make things right with Christ and the congregation. Unless treated, the effects of your corporate pain will linger and begin to hinder ministry effectiveness, regardless of who leads the church.

Action Point: If your church is wounded, seek the Lord in regard to what is necessary to bring corporate healing to your congregation. Ask Him to give you the courage it will take to walk through such a process honestly and effectively. Avail yourselves of the consulting services Blessing Point Ministries offers to help you in this regard.

Little Evidence of Historical Crises (Score 16-20) This is a great blessing to be celebrated. Rare is the church in existence more than ten years which has not faced such a crisis. Your church appears free of major pain, and it's something for which you should be tremendously thankful! But a clear history does not mean a clear future. Make sure you as leaders are staying prepared to face such events with wisdom and sensitivity.

Action Point: Become familiar with the principles of *Healing the Heart of Your Church* by Ken Quick and reconciliation before you need them. Ask God to give you the grace to deal with conflict or crises (when they do come) in a way He can bless. Many churches languish for having failed to do so.

GENERAL ASSESSEMENTS:

Low Overall Score (50 or less) Your church is likely experiencing, or, has experienced in the past, a high degree of congregational pain and you need to do something about it *immediately* to get your church healthy again.

Churches that score in the 25-50 range are in dire need of corporate healing. Such churches manifest a variety of symptoms which often seem bewildering to the people who lead them. Symptoms can include irrational levels of resistance to change, anxiety about the future, distrust between lay and professional leaders and between leaders and congregation, all of which makes leading difficult if not impossible. Schisms form around lightning-rod issues— worship, associate staff, the pastor. Offenses become magnified. Bad behavior often precedes splits or exoduses. Those who visit the church don't stay long. Church members "acclimatize" to the environment and see all this as "normal." Unaddressed, these painful symptoms usually increase in intensity and frequency.

Leaders and members often misdiagnose the true nature of their corporate problems and blame the pastor, staff member(s) or particular lay leaders. Corporate meetings are dreaded. Leaders often attribute the problems to the inadequate policies or ineffective programs. They sense that something is wrong, but don't quite know what it is.

Shepherds who minister in these contexts often feel like failures, and they blame themselves or others for the church's stalemate. Their personal health often suffers, sometimes severely. They carry heavy burdens and, despite their best efforts to make progress, they keep slipping back. The pressures of leadership also bear down on the pastor's spouse and children.

How We Can Help: We suggest you consider our consulting

THE CHURCHSCAN INVENTORY

services. We can help your church work through issues that need attention. Blessing Point's consultants use a biblically-based, spiritually-sensitive, systemic approach to recurring church problems and corporate pain. We turn a church's corporate focus back to the Lord of their church and believe that Christ will give direction, not only to the individuals within a church, but to the whole church body to heal it. We help a church learn to listen to Jesus speak to their church corporately. Our consultants know the right questions to ask. They will assist church leaders in mapping the church's history and help you hear clearly from Christ regarding responses that fit you and your church to address the root problems and break the cycle of dysfunction.

A Biblical Process: Blessing Point consultants help define a biblical process with your church leaders to determine what has damaged the "tapestry" of your church. We believe that the Lord Jesus Christ always makes what is wrong very clear. It is His church, purchased by His blood, so He has a vested interest in its health.

The problem is that church leaders often focus only on the present symptoms and not on the past where the root problems began. That's because leaders feel powerless to "fix" those past issues. They must learn how to diagnose the signals Christ sends them through the episodes of corporate pain in their history and how to deal with those past, unresolved issues.

Medium Overall Score (51-75) You need to address the causes of your problems and work toward strengthening your church - *before things get worse.*

Churches scoring in the 51-75 range exhibit a mix of healthy and unhealthy traits, where the key for leaders is to assess honestly the frequency and direction of them, i.e. are they getting worse? The lower your score, the more likely you are experiencing a decrease in fruitfulness and an increase in corporate pain.

Toward the top of the scoring, problems show up intermittently, perhaps with years or decades between major crises. The level of pain in your church appears tolerable on most days. Good things still happen in your congregation.

Again the direction and frequency of pain and ministry frustration needs to be monitored. Monitoring is important because most leaders find corporate introspection distasteful or unproductive. However God requires us as His children to consider our ways to see if they are pleasing to Him. Inattention to the condition of your church body can leave you vulnerable. Wise leaders learn to ask "Where are we experiencing corporate pain right now?" and to give honest answers to the question.

Many of the traits identified in the survey relate to dysfunction in a church's spiritual and relational processes. Dysfunction may not appear obvious on Sunday morning, but becomes evident in leader relationships and how issues play out behind the scenes.

Be honest about your church. You are in grave danger if competition with other churches or church leaders, fear of blame or fear of failure prevents honesty. No church is perfect and acknowledging that fact about one's own church is a healthy step.

The temptation to overlook pain in one's church is strong. You can blame the pain on Satan, think of it as normal, or pray to get through it. However, if the pain is a signal of corporate discipline from the Lord of your church, then all of those "answers" will fall short of solving what you face. You need to hear from Him and do what He says about it.

How We Can Help: Blessing Point has consultants available to churches in need of advice and counsel, either short or long term. We will come in for a one day seminar or facilitate your church through our Healing the Heart of Your Church process.

THE CHURCHSCAN INVENTORY

If you feel you need more confirmation of a need to repair the fabric of your church, read *Healing the Heart of Your Church* or *Body Aches* by Dr. Kenneth Quick. These resources will help you decide if you need to move forward with a reparative work.

If your church is healthy enough, you may be able to lead yourselves through the corporate healing process using our *Healing the Heart of Your Church Facilitator's Guide and Participant Workbooks.* However, sometimes when key players in the church are too enmeshed with the situation to be objective, an outside consultant can help. Consider having one of our biblically-based, spiritually-sensitive facilitators come alongside your leadership and guide you through this process.

A Biblical Process: Blessing Point consultants help define a biblical process with your church leaders to determine what has damaged your church. We believe that the Lord Jesus Christ always makes what is wrong very clear. It is His church, purchased by His blood, so He has a vested interest in its health.

The problem is that church leaders often focus only on the present symptoms and not on the past where the root problems began. That's because leaders feel powerless to "fix" those past issues. They must learn how to diagnose the signals Christ sends them through the episodes of corporate pain in their history and how to deal with those past, unresolved issues.

High Overall Score (76-100) Your church, like most healthy churches, experiences occasional episodes of difficulty and challenge, but these are normal challenges. Consider investing in your leadership team to keep your church healthy.

Churches scoring in the 76-100 range enjoy spiritual and numerical health. Your church provides a wonderful illustration of the grace of God to your community! There may be individual categories of this assessment that need attention—you are not perfect—but overall you are doing things the right way. This is not time to grow complacent. Invest in the wellbeing of your leadership and congregation and prepare for the day when you may need to deal with corporate pain.

Challenges will come to your church as they do to all churches. But with those challenges come opportunities as was the case with the church of Philadelphia in Rev. 3:7-13. In fact, churches that overcome obstacles are usually gifted with greater opportunities for the kingdom. Be alert to the church health risks as communicated by the questions of this survey. And take the time to equip your leaders to protect your church from such dangers. Consider studying *The Eighth Letter* (ChurchSmart 2014) by Mark Barnard and Ken Quick. It will give your leaders insight into how to monitor and strengthen the systemic health of your church.

How Can We Help: Blessing Point has trained consultants available to equip your church leaders to ask the right questions to effectively monitor and protect your church's corporate health. Consider having us come for a day of training for your leaders.

OTHER RESOURCES TO HELP YOUR CHURCH

Available from churchsmart.com and amazon.com

Healing the Heart of Your Church: How Church Leaders Can Break the Pattern of Historic Corporate Dysfunction, by Dr. Kenneth Quick

Healing the Heart of Your Church Facilitator and Participant Guides, by Mark Barnard and Dr. Kenneth Quick.

Sustaining the Heart of Your Church: Twenty Exercises to Help Church Leaders Overcome Lingering Corporate Dysfunction, by Mark Barnard

Body Aches: Experiencing and Responding to God's Discipline of Your Church, by Dr. Kenneth Quick

Screwtape's Promotion, by E.H. Muse

The Eighth Letter – Jesus Still Speaks! What is He saying to your church?, by Mark Barnard and Dr. Kenneth Quick

The Path of Revival: Restoring Our Nation One Church at a Time, by Mark Barnard

For more helpful resources visit Blessing Point Ministries - blessingpoint.org

ACKNOWLEDGMENTS

Three people deserve a big THANK YOU for their help with this project. Ken Quick's encouragement and editing were invaluable, as always. His willingness to allow others, like myself, to build on his work evidences his incredibly warm and gracious spirit. Debbie Smith used her editing skills to help clean up an early version of the manuscript for this book. And Dave Wetzler added counsel and direction in the manuscript's latter development that I dearly appreciate.

ABOUT THE AUTHOR

Rev. Mark Barnard serves as President of Blessing Point Ministries, which works to heal churches that have been wounded by painful crises. Mark has a BA in Bible and an MA in Pastoral Studies. He authored *The Path of Revival* and coauthored *The Eighth Letter* as well as the *Healing the Heart of Your Church Facilitator's Guide*. Mark previously served in a variety of pastoral and teaching roles. He, his wife Jeannie, and their children reside in Peachtree City, GA.

For speaking or consulting needs contact us at
info@blessingpoint.org

NOTES

NOTES

NOTES

NOTES

NOTES

NOTES

NOTES

NOTES

NOTES

NOTES

NOTES

NOTES

NOTES

NOTES

NOTES

NOTES

Made in the USA
Charleston, SC
30 January 2017